SING

The Book of Psalms

Today's English Version

SING

The Book of Psalms

Today's English Version

AMERICAN BIBLE SOCIETY
New York

THE PSALMS
in Today's English Version

The Psalms were originally published as

PSALMS FOR MODERN MAN

ENG. PSALMS TEV 560P-04456
ABS-1984-30,000-6,121,000-WE-33-(4R)

Printed In The United States of America.

PREFACE

THE BOOK OF PSALMS is the hymnbook and prayer book of the Bible. Composed by different authors over a long period of time, these hymns and prayers were collected and used by the people of Israel in their worship, and eventually this collection was included in their Holy Scriptures.

These religious poems are of many kinds: there are hymns of praise and worship of God; prayers for help, protection, and salvation; pleas for forgiveness; songs of thanksgiving for God's blessings; and petitions for the punishment of enemies. These prayers are personal and national; some portray the most intimate feelings of one person, while others represent the needs and feelings of all the people of God.

Many of the Psalms are quoted in the New Testament, and such passages as Mary's song of praise (Luke 1.46-55), Zechariah's prophecy (Luke 1.68-79), and Simeon's prayer of thanksgiving (Luke 2.29-32) reflect the language and style of the psalms. They were used by Jesus, quoted by the writers of the New Testament, and became the treasured book of worship of the Christian Church from its very beginning.

This translation of *The Psalms* attempts to represent the meaning of the Hebrew text as faithfully as possible, and at the same time convey something of the grace and beauty of the original poetry. The basic poetic structure of the Psalms consists of a statement which is repeated, in a modified fashion, in the next line. Sometimes this parallelism is continued over several lines. The possible variations are almost unlimited, and the reader who is aware of them will discover new beauty in the Psalms. In addition, unusual words and figurative expressions help create and sustain a poetic atmosphere.

Ancient Hebrew poetry did not have rhyme, and the meter was quite different from what is commonly used in English. This translation has been made in free verse, and the translators have tried to put the Psalms in easy-flowing, rhythmical lines that can be effective in public worship as well as in private devotion.

Today's English Version is a distinctively new translation, which does not conform to traditional vocabulary or style. It seeks instead to express the meaning of the Hebrew text in words and forms accepted as standard by people everywhere who employ English as a means of communication.

Where there is general agreement that the Hebrew text presents unresolved difficulties in interpretation, this translation employs the evidence of other ancient texts or follows present-day scholarly concensus. All such modifications are identified in footnotes. Other footnotes give information designed to help the reader understand the meaning of the text, especially where ancient beliefs are expressed or alluded to.

The Bible in Today's English Version is called the *Good News Bible* and is available from the American Bible Society.

THE PSALMS

Outline of Contents

The 150 psalms are grouped into five collections, or
books, as follows:

BOOK ONE
(Psalms 1—41)

True Happiness

1 Happy are those
    who reject the advice of evil men,
  who do not follow the example of
      sinners
  or join those who have no use for
      God.
² Instead, they find joy in obeying the
      Law of the LORD,
  and they study it day and night.
³ They are like trees that grow beside a
      stream,
  that bear fruit at the right time,
  and whose leaves do not dry up.
  They succeed in everything they do.

⁴ But evil men are not like this at all;
  they are like straw that the wind
      blows away.
⁵ Sinners will be condemned by God
  and kept apart from God's own
      people.
⁶ The righteous are guided and protected
      by the LORD,
  but the evil are on the way to their
      doom.

1

God's Chosen King

2 Why do the nations plan rebellion?
   Why do people make their useless
       plots?
² Their kings revolt,
     their rulers plot together against the
         LORD
     and against the king he chose.
³ "Let us free ourselves from their rule,"
       they say;
     "let us throw off their control."

⁴ From his throne in heaven the Lord
       laughs
     and mocks their feeble plans.
⁵ Then he warns them in anger
     and terrifies them with his fury.
⁶ "On Zion,ᵃ my sacred hill," he says,
     "I have installed my king."

⁷ "I will announce," says the king, "what
       the LORD has declared.
     He said to me: 'You are my son;
     today I have become your father.
⁸ Ask, and I will give you all the nations;
     the whole earth will be yours.
⁹ You will break them with an iron rod;
     you will shatter them in pieces like a
         clay pot.' "

¹⁰ Now listen to this warning, you kings;
     learn this lesson, you rulers of the
         world:
¹¹ Serve the LORD with fear;
     tremble ¹² and bow down to him;ᵇ

ᵃ ZION: *The term "Zion" (originally a designation for "David's City,"
the Jebusite stronghold captured by King David's forces) was later
extended in meaning to refer to the hill on which the Temple stood.*
ᵇ *Probable text* tremble . . . him; *some other possible texts* with
trembling kiss his feet *and* with trembling kiss the Son *and* tremble
and kiss the mighty one; *Hebrew unclear.*

or else his anger will be quickly
    aroused,
  and you will suddenly die.
Happy are all who go to him for
    protection.

Morning Prayer for Help[c]

3 I have so many enemies, LORD,
    so many who turn against me!
[2] They talk about me and say,
  "God will not help him."

[3] But you, O LORD, are always my shield
    from danger;
  you give me victory
  and restore my courage.

You, O LORD, are always my shield from danger. (3.3)

[4] I call to the LORD for help,
    and from his sacred hill[d] he answers
    me.

[c] HEBREW TITLE: *A psalm by David, after he ran away from his son
Absalom.*   [d] SACRED HILL: *See 2.6.*

⁵ I lie down and sleep,
    and all night long the Lord protects
      me.
⁶ I am not afraid of the thousands of
      enemies
    who surround me on every side.

⁷ Come, Lord! Save me, my God!
    You punish all my enemies
      and leave them powerless to harm
      me.
⁸ Victory comes from the Lord—
    may he bless his people.

Evening Prayer for Help*

4 Answer me when I pray,
    O God, my defender!
When I was in trouble, you helped me.
    Be kind to me now and hear my
      prayer.

² How long will you people insult me?
    How long will you love what is
      worthless
    and go after what is false?

³ Remember that the Lord has chosen
      the righteous for his own,
    and he hears me when I call to him.

⁴ Tremble with fear and stop sinning;
    think deeply about this,
    when you lie in silence on your beds.
⁵ Offer the right sacrifices to the Lord,
    and put your trust in him.

⁶ There are many who pray:
    "Give us more blessings, O Lord.
    Look on us with kindness!"
⁷ But the joy that you have given me
    is more than they will ever have
    with all their grain and wine.

* HEBREW TITLE: *A psalm by David.*

⁸ When I lie down, I go to sleep in peace;
   you alone, O LORD, keep me
   perfectly safe.

A Prayer for Protection ⁱ

5 Listen to my words, O LORD,
      and hear my sighs.
² Listen to my cry for help,
   my God and king!

   I pray to you, O LORD;
³   you hear my voice in the morning;
   at sunrise I offer my prayerᵍ
      and wait for your answer.

⁴ You are not a God who is pleased with
      wrongdoing;
   you allow no evil in your presence.
⁵ You cannot stand the sight of proud
      men;
   you hate all wicked people.
⁶ You destroy all liars
   and despise violent, deceitful men.

⁷ But because of your great love
      I can come into your house;
   I can worship in your holy Temple
      and bow down to you in reverence.
⁸ LORD, I have so many enemies!
      Lead me to do your will;
   make your way plain for me to
      follow.

⁹ What my enemies say can never be
      trusted;
   they only want to destroy.
   Their words are flattering and smooth,
      but full of deadly deceit.
¹⁰ Condemn and punish them, O God;
   may their own plots cause their ruin.

ⁱ HEBREW TITLE: *A psalm by David.*   ᵍ prayer; *or* sacrifice.

Drive them out of your presence
because of their many sins
and their rebellion against you.

11 But all who find safety in you will
rejoice;
they can always sing for joy.
Protect those who love you;
because of you they are truly happy.
12 You bless those who obey you, LORD;
your love protects them like a shield.

A Prayer for Help in Time of Trouble[h]

6 LORD, don't be angry and rebuke
me!
Don't punish me in your anger!
2 I am worn out, O LORD; have pity on
me!
Give me strength; I am completely
exhausted
3 and my whole being is deeply
troubled.
How long, O LORD, will you wait to
help me?

4 Come and save me, LORD;
in your mercy rescue me from death.
5 In the world of the dead you are not
remembered;
no one can praise you there.

6 I am worn out with grief;
every night my bed is damp from my
weeping;
my pillow is soaked with tears.
7 I can hardly see;
my eyes are so swollen
from the weeping caused by my
enemies.

[h] HEBREW TITLE: *A psalm by David.*

⁸ Keep away from me, you evil men!
The LORD hears my weeping;
⁹   he listens to my cry for help
and will answer my prayer.
¹⁰ My enemies will know the bitter shame
of defeat;
in sudden confusion they will be
driven away.

A Prayer for Justice

7 O LORD, my God, I come to you for
protection;
rescue me and save me from all who
pursue me,
² or else like a lion they will carry me off
where no one can save me,
and there they will tear me to pieces.

³⁻⁴ O LORD, my God, if I have wronged
anyone,
if I have betrayed a friend
or without cause done violence to my
enemy ʲ
if I have done any of these things—
⁵ then let my enemies pursue me and
catch me,
let them cut me down and kill me
and leave me lifeless on the ground!

⁶ Rise in your anger, O LORD!
Stand up against the fury of my
enemies;
rouse yourself and help me!
Justice is what you demand,
⁷   so bring together all the peoples
around you,
and rule over them from above.ᵏ

ⁱ HEBREW TITLE: *A song which David sang to the LORD because of
Cush the Benjaminite.*   ʲ *without cause done violence to my enemy;
or shown mercy to someone who wronged me unjustly.*
ᵏ *Probable text* rule over them from above; *Hebrew* return above
over them.

⁸ You are the judge of all mankind.
    Judge in my favor, O Lᴏʀᴅ;
    you know that I am innocent.
⁹ You are a righteous God
    and judge our thoughts and desires.
  Stop the wickedness of evil men
    and reward those who are good.

¹⁰ God is my protector;
    he saves those who obey him.
¹¹ God is a righteous judge
    and always condemns the wicked.
¹² If they do not change their ways,
    God will sharpen his sword.
  He bends his bow and makes it ready;
¹³   he takes up his deadly weapons
    and aims his burning arrows.

¹⁴ See how wicked people think up evil;
    they plan trouble and practice
      deception.
¹⁵ But in the traps they set for others,
    they themselves get caught.
¹⁶ So they are punished by their own evil
    and are hurt by their own violence.

¹⁷ I thank the Lᴏʀᴅ for his justice;
    I sing praises to the Lᴏʀᴅ, the Most
      High.

God's Glory and Man's Dignity[1]

8 O Lᴏʀᴅ, our Lord,
    your greatness is seen in all the
      world!
  Your praise reaches up to the heavens;
²   it is sung by children and babies.
  You are safe and secure from all your
    enemies;
    you stop anyone who opposes you.

[1] ʜᴇʙʀᴇᴡ ᴛɪᴛʟᴇ: *A psalm by David.*

Your greatness is seen in all the world! (8.9)

3 When I look at the sky, which you have
　　made,
　　　at the moon and the stars, which you
　　　　set in their places—
4 what is man, that you think of him;
　　　mere man, that you care for him?

5 Yet you made him inferior only to
　　yourself;ᵐ
　　　you crowned him with glory and
　　　　honor.
6 You appointed him ruler over
　　everything you made;
　　　you placed him over all creation:
7 　sheep and cattle, and the wild
　　　animals too;
8 　the birds and the fish
　　　and the creatures in the seas.

9 O LORD, our Lord,
　　your greatness is seen in all the
　　　world!

ᵐ *yourself;* or *the gods,* or *the angels.*

Thanksgiving to God for His Justice[n]

9 I will praise you, LORD, with all my
heart;
I will tell of all the wonderful things
you have done.
[2] I will sing with joy because of you.
I will sing praise to you, Almighty
God.

[3] My enemies turn back when you
appear;
they fall down and die.
[4] You are fair and honest in your
judgments,
and you have judged in my favor.

[5] You have condemned the heathen
and destroyed the wicked;
they will be remembered no more.
[6] Our enemies are finished forever;
you have destroyed their cities,
and they are completely forgotten.

[7] But the LORD is king forever;
he has set up his throne for judgment.
[8] He rules the world with righteousness;
he judges the nations with justice.

[9] The LORD is a refuge for the oppressed,
a place of safety in times of trouble.
[10] Those who know you, LORD, will trust
you;
you do not abandon anyone who
comes to you.

[11] Sing praise to the LORD, who rules in
Zion!
Tell every nation what he has done!

HEBREW TITLE: *A psalm by David.*

¹² God remembers those who suffer;
> he does not forget their cry,
> and he punishes those who wrong
> them.

¹³ Be merciful to me, O LORD!
> See the sufferings my enemies cause
> me!
> Rescue me from death, O LORD,
¹⁴   that I may stand before the people of
> Jerusalem
> and tell them all the things for which
> I praise you.
> I will rejoice because you saved me.

¹⁵ The heathen have dug a pit and fallen
> in;
> they have been caught in their own
> trap.
¹⁶ The LORD has revealed himself by his
> righteous judgments,
> and the wicked are trapped by their
> own deeds.

¹⁷ Death is the destiny of all the wicked,
> of all those who reject God.
¹⁸ The needy will not always be neglected;
> the hope of the poor will not be
> crushed forever.

¹⁹ Come, LORD! Do not let men defy you!
> Bring the heathen before you
> and pronounce judgment on them.
²⁰ Make them afraid, O LORD;
> make them know that they are only
> mortal beings.

A Prayer for Justice

10 Why are you so far away, O
> LORD?
> Why do you hide yourself when we
> are in trouble?

² The wicked are proud and persecute
the poor;
catch them in the traps they have
made.

³ The wicked man is proud of his evil
desires;
the greedy man curses and rejects the
LORD.
⁴ A wicked man does not care about the
LORD;
in his pride he thinks that God
doesn't matter.

⁵ A wicked man succeeds in everything.
He cannot understand God's
judgments;
he sneers at his enemies.
⁶ He says to himself, "I will never fail;
I will never be in trouble."
⁷ His speech is filled with curses, lies,
and threats;
he is quick to speak hateful, evil
words.

⁸ He hides himself in the villages,
waiting to murder innocent people.
He spies on his helpless victims;
⁹   he waits in his hiding place like a
lion.
He lies in wait for the poor;
he catches them in his trap and drags
them away.

¹⁰ The helpless victims lie crushed;
brute strength has defeated them.
¹¹ The wicked man says to himself, "God
doesn't care!
He has closed his eyes and will never
see me!"

¹² O LORD, punish those wicked men!
    Remember those who are suffering!
¹³ How can a wicked man despise God
    and say to himself, "He will not
        punish me"?

¹⁴ But you do see; you take notice of
        trouble and suffering
    and are always ready to help.
  The helpless man commits himself to
        you;
    you have always helped the needy.

¹⁵ Break the power of wicked and evil
        men;
    punish them for the wrong they have
        done
    until they do it no more.

¹⁶ The LORD is king forever and ever.
    Those who worship other gods
    will vanish from his land.

¹⁷ You will listen, O LORD, to the prayers
        of the lowly;
    you will give them courage.
¹⁸ You will hear the cries of the oppressed
        and the orphans;
    you will judge in their favor,
    so that mortal men may cause terror
        no more.

Confidence in the LORD ᵒ

11 I trust in the LORD for safety.
    How foolish of you to say to
        me,
"Fly away like a bird to the mountains,ᵖ

ᵒ HEBREW TITLE: *By David.*   ᵖ *Some ancient translations* like a bird
to the mountains; *Hebrew* bird, to your *(plural)* mountains.

²   because the wicked have drawn their
     bows and aimed their arrows
   to shoot from the shadows at good
     men.
³ There is nothing a good man can do
     when everything falls apart."

⁴ The LORD is in his holy temple;
     he has his throne in heaven.
He watches people everywhere
     and knows what they are doing.
⁵ He examines the good and the wicked
      alike;
     the lawless he hates with all his heart.

⁶ He sends down flaming coals*ᵃ* and
     burning sulfur on the wicked;
   he punishes them with scorching
     winds.
⁷ The LORD is righteous and loves good
     deeds;
   those who do them will live in his
     presence.

A Prayer for Help*ʳ*

12   Help us, LORD!
      There is not a good man left;
   honest men can no longer be found.
² All of them lie to one another;
     they deceive each other with flattery.

³ Silence those flattering tongues, O
     LORD!
   Close those boastful mouths that say,
⁴ "With our words we get what we want.
   We will say what we wish,
   and no one can stop us."

ᵃ One ancient translation coals; *Hebrew* traps.   *ʳ* HEBREW TITLE: *A psalm by David.*

5 "But now I will come," says the LORD,
   "because the needy are oppressed
   and the persecuted groan in pain.
I will give them the security they long
      for."

6 The promises of the LORD can be
      trusted;
   they are as genuine as silver
   refined seven times in the furnace.

7-8 Wicked men are everywhere,
    and everyone praises what is evil.
Keep us always safe, O LORD,
    and preserve us from such people.

A Prayer for Help[5]

13 How much longer will you forget
   me, LORD? Forever?
How much longer will you hide
   yourself from me?
2 How long must I endure trouble?
   How long will sorrow fill my heart
      day and night?
   How long will my enemies triumph
      over me?

3 Look at me, O LORD my God, and
      answer me.
   Restore my strength; don't let me die.
4 Don't let my enemies say, "We have
      defeated him."
   Don't let them gloat over my
      downfall.

5 I rely on your constant love;
   I will be glad, because you will
      rescue me.
6 I will sing to you, O LORD,
   because you have been good to me.

5 HEBREW TITLE: A psalm by David.

The Wickedness of Men[/]
(Psalm 53)

14 Fools say to themselves,
     "There is no God!"
They are all corrupt,
     and they have done terrible things;
     there is no one who does what is
          right.

[2] The LORD looks down from heaven at
          mankind
     to see if there are any who are wise,
     any who worship him.
[3] But they have all gone wrong;
     they are all equally bad.
Not one of them does what is right,
     not a single one.

[4] "Don't they know?" asks the LORD.
     "Are all these evildoers ignorant?
They live by robbing my people,
     and they never pray to me."

[5] But then they will be terrified,
     for God is with those who obey him.
[6] Evildoers frustrate the plans of the
          humble man,
     but the LORD is his protection.

[7] How I pray that victory
     will come to Israel from Zion.
How happy the people of Israel will be
     when the LORD makes them
          prosperous again!

What God Requires[u]

15 LORD, who may enter your
          Temple?
Who may worship on Zion, your
     sacred hill?[v]

[/] HEBREW TITLE: *By David.*   [u] HEBREW TITLE: *A psalm by David.*
[v] SACRED HILL: *See 2.6.*

2 A person who obeys God in everything
    and always does what is right,
  whose words are true and sincere,
3   and who does not slander others.
  He does no wrong to his friends
    nor spreads rumors about his
      neighbors.
4 He despises those whom God rejects,
    but honors those who obey the LORD.
  He always does what he promises,
    no matter how much it may cost.
5 He makes loans without charging
      interest
    and cannot be bribed to testify
      against the innocent.

  Whoever does these things will always
    be secure.

A Prayer of Confidence [w]

16 Protect me, O God; I trust in you
       for safety.
2 I say to the LORD, "You are my Lord;
    all the good things I have come from
      you."

3 How excellent are the LORD's faithful
      people!
  My greatest pleasure is to be with
    them.

4 Those who rush to other gods
    bring many troubles on themselves.[x]
  I will not take part in their sacrifices;
    I will not worship their gods.

5 You, LORD, are all I have,
    and you give me all I need;
  my future is in your hands.

---

[w] HEBREW TITLE: *A psalm by David.*   [x] *Probable text* Those . . .
themselves; *Hebrew unclear.*

⁶ How wonderful are your gifts to me;
    how good they are!

⁷ I praise the LORD, because he guides
        me,
    and in the night my conscience warns
        me.
⁸ I am always aware of the LORD's
        presence;
    he is near, and nothing can shake me.

⁹ And so I am thankful and glad,
    and I feel completely secure,
¹⁰ because you protect me from the power
        of death.
    I have served you faithfully,
        and you will not abandon me to the
        world of the dead.

¹¹ You will show me the path that leads
        to life;
    your presence fills me with joy
    and brings me pleasure forever.

The Prayer of an Innocent Man ʸ

17 Listen, O LORD, to my plea for
        justice;
    pay attention to my cry for help!
    Listen to my honest prayer.
² You will judge in my favor,
    because you know what is right.

³ You know my heart.
    You have come to me at night;
    you have examined me completely
    and found no evil desire in me.
    I speak no evil, ⁴ as others do;
    I have obeyed your command
    and have not followed paths of
        violence.

ʸ HEBREW TITLE: *A prayer by David.*

⁵ I have always walked in your way
and have never strayed from it.

⁶ I pray to you, O God, because you
answer me;
so turn to me and listen to my words.
⁷ Reveal your wonderful love and save
me;
at your side I am safe from my
enemies.

⁸ Protect me as you would your very
eyes;
hide me in the shadow of your wings
⁹   from the attacks of the wicked.

Deadly enemies surround me;
¹⁰   they have no pity and speak proudly.
¹¹ They are around me now, wherever I
turn,
watching for a chance to pull me
down.
¹² They are like lions, waiting for me,
wanting to tear me to pieces.

¹³ Come, LORD! Oppose my enemies and
defeat them!
Save me from the wicked by your
sword;
¹⁴   save me from those who in this life
have all they want.
Punish them with the sufferings you
have stored up for them;
may there be enough for their
children
and some left over for their children's
children!

¹⁵ But I will see you, because I have done
no wrong;
and when I awake, your presence will
fill me with joy.

David's Song of Victory [z]

(2 Samuel 22.1-51)

18 How I love you, LORD!
You are my defender.

2 The LORD is my protector;
he is my strong fortress.
My God is my protection,
and with him I am safe.
He protects me like a shield;
he defends me and keeps me safe.
3 I call to the LORD,
and he saves me from my enemies.
Praise the LORD!

4 The danger of death was all around me;
the waves of destruction rolled over
me.
5 The danger of death was around me,
and the grave set its trap for me.
6 In my trouble I called to the LORD;
I called to my God for help.
In his temple he heard my voice;
he listened to my cry for help.

7 Then the earth trembled and shook;
the foundations of the mountains
rocked and quivered,
because God was angry.
8 Smoke poured out of his nostrils,
a consuming flame and burning coals
from his mouth.
9 He tore the sky open and came down
with a dark cloud under his feet.
10 He flew swiftly on his winged creature; [x]
he traveled on the wings of the wind.
11 He covered himself with darkness;
thick clouds, full of water,
surrounded him.

---

[z] HEBREW TITLE: *The words that David, the LORD's servant, sang to
the LORD on the day the LORD saved him from Saul and all his other
enemies.* [x] WINGED CREATURES: *See Word List.*

¹² Hailstones and flashes of fire
    came from the lightning before him
    and broke through the dark clouds.

¹³ Then the LORD thundered from the sky;
    and the voice of the Most High was
        heard.ᵃ
¹⁴ He shot his arrows and scattered his
        enemies;
    with flashes of lightning he sent them
        running.
¹⁵ The floor of the ocean was laid bare,
    and the foundations of the earth were
        uncovered,
    when you rebuked your enemies, LORD,
    and roared at them in anger.

¹⁶ The LORD reached down from above
    and took hold of me;
    he pulled me out of the deep waters.
¹⁷ He rescued me from my powerful
        enemies
    and from all those who hate me—
    they were too strong for me.
¹⁸ When I was in trouble, they attacked
        me,
    but the LORD protected me.
¹⁹ He helped me out of danger;
    he saved me because he was pleased
        with me.

²⁰ The LORD rewards me because I do
        what is right;
    he blesses me because I am innocent.
²¹ I have obeyed the law of the LORD;
    I have not turned away from my
        God.
²² I have observed all his laws;
    I have not disobeyed his commands.

ᵃ *One ancient translation (and see 2 S 22.14)* was heard; *Hebrew* was
heard hailstones and flashes of fire.

²³ He knows that I am faultless,
   that I have kept myself from doing
      wrong.
²⁴ And so he rewards me because I do
      what is right,
   because he knows that I am innocent.

²⁵ O LORD, you are faithful to those who
      are faithful to you;
   completely good to those who are
      perfect.
²⁶ You are pure to those who are pure,
   but hostile to those who are wicked.
²⁷ You save those who are humble,
   but you humble those who are proud.

²⁸ O LORD, you give me light;
   you dispel my darkness.
²⁹ You give me strength to attack my
      enemies
   and power to overcome their
      defenses.

³⁰ This God—how perfect are his deeds!
   How dependable his words!
   He is like a shield
   for all who seek his protection.
³¹ The LORD alone is God;
   God alone is our defense.
³² He is the God who makes me strong,
   who makes my pathway safe.
³³ He makes me sure-footed as a deer;
   he keeps me safe on the mountains.
³⁴ He trains me for battle,
   so that I can use the strongest bow.

³⁵ O LORD, you protect me and save me;
   your care has made me great,
   and your power has kept me safe.
³⁶ You have kept me from being captured,
   and I have never fallen.
³⁷ I pursue my enemies and catch them;
   I do not stop until I destroy them.

[38] I strike them down, and they cannot
rise;
they lie defeated before me.
[39] You give me strength for the battle
and victory over my enemies.
[40] You make my enemies run from me;
I destroy those who hate me.
[41] They cry for help, but no one saves
them;
they call to the LORD, but he does
not answer.
[42] I crush them, so that they become like
dust
which the wind blows away.
I trample on them like mud in the
streets.

[43] You saved me from a rebellious people
and made me ruler over the nations;
people I did not know have now
become my subjects.
[44] Foreigners bow before me;
when they hear me, they obey.
[45] They lose their courage
and come trembling from their
fortresses.

[46] The LORD lives! Praise my defender!
Proclaim the greatness of the God
who saves me.
[47] He gives me victory over my enemies;
he subdues the nations under me
[48] and saves me from my foes.

O LORD, you give me victory over my
enemies
and protect me from violent men.
[49] And so I praise you among the nations;
I sing praises to you.

[50] God gives great victories to his king;
he shows constant love to the one he
has chosen,
to David and his descendants forever.

God's Glory in Creation[b]

19 How clearly the sky reveals
God's glory!
How plainly it shows what he has
done!
[2] Each day announces it to the following
day;
each night repeats it to the next.
[3] No speech or words are used,
no sound is heard;
[4] yet their message[c] goes out to all the
world
and is heard to the ends of the earth.
God made a home in the sky for the
sun;
[5] it comes out in the morning like a
happy bridegroom,
like an athlete eager to run a race.
[6] It starts at one end of the sky
and goes across to the other.
Nothing can hide from its heat.

The Law of the LORD

[7] The law of the LORD is perfect;
it gives new strength.
The commands of the LORD are
trustworthy,
giving wisdom to those who lack it.
[8] The laws of the LORD are right,
and those who obey them are happy.
The commands of the LORD are just
and give understanding to the mind.
[9] Reverence for the LORD is good;
it will continue forever.
The judgments of the LORD are just;
they are always fair.
[10] They are more desirable than the finest
gold;
they are sweeter than the purest
honey.

[b] HEBREW TITLE: *A psalm by David.* [c] *Some ancient translations*
message; *Hebrew* line.

¹¹ They give knowledge to me, your
       servant;
   I am rewarded for obeying them.

¹² No one can see his own errors;
   deliver me, LORD, from hidden faults!
¹³ Keep me safe, also, from willful sins;
   don't let them rule over me.
Then I shall be perfect
   and free from the evil of sin.

¹⁴ May my words and my thoughts be
      acceptable to you,
   O LORD, my refuge and my redeemer!

A Prayer for Victory[d]

20 May the LORD answer you when
      you are in trouble!
May the God of Jacob protect you!
² May he send you help from his Temple
   and give you aid from Mount Zion.
³ May he accept all your offerings
   and be pleased with all your
      sacrifices.
⁴ May he give you what you desire
   and make all your plans succeed.
⁵ Then we will shout for joy over your
      victory
   and celebrate your triumph by
      praising our God.
May the LORD answer all your
      requests.

⁶ Now I know that the LORD gives
      victory to his chosen king;
   he answers him from his holy heaven
   and by his power gives him great
      victories.

[d] HEBREW TITLE: *A psalm by David.*

⁷ Some trust in their war chariots
    and others in their horses,
        but we trust in the power of the
            LORD our God.
⁸ Such people will stumble and fall,
    but we will rise and stand firm.

⁹ Give victory to the king, O LORD;
    answer*e* us when we call.

Praise for Victoryᶠ

21 The king is glad, O LORD,
        because you gave him
            strength;
    he rejoices because you made him
        victorious.
² You have given him his heart's desire;
    you have answered his request.

³ You came to him with great blessings
    and set a crown of gold on his head.
⁴ He asked for life, and you gave it,
    a long and lasting life.

⁵ His glory is great because of your help;
    you have given him fame and
        majesty.
⁶ Your blessings are with him forever,
    and your presence fills him with joy.

⁷ The king trusts in the LORD Almighty;
    and because of the LORD's constant
        love
    he will always be secure.
⁸ The king will capture all his enemies;
    he will capture everyone who hates
        him.
⁹ He will destroy them like a blazing fire
    when he appears.

e Some ancient translations answer; *Hebrew* he will answer.
ᶠ HEBREW TITLE: *A psalm by David.*

The LORD will devour them in his
    anger,
and fire will consume them.
[10] None of their descendants will survive;
    the king will kill them all.

[11] They make their plans, and plot against
    him,
but they will not succeed.
[12] He will shoot his arrows at them
    and make them turn and run.

[13] We praise you, LORD, for your great
    strength!
We will sing and praise your power.

A Cry of Anguish and a Song of Praise[R]

22 My God, my God, why have you
        abandoned me?
I have cried desperately for help,
    but still it does not come.
[2] During the day I call to you, my God,
    but you do not answer;
I call at night,
    but get no rest.
[3] But you are enthroned as the Holy
    One,
the one whom Israel praises.
[4] Our ancestors put their trust in you;
    they trusted you, and you saved them.
[5] They called to you and escaped from
    danger;
they trusted you and were not
    disappointed.

[6] But I am no longer a man; I am a
    worm,
despised and scorned by everyone!
[7] All who see me make fun of me;
    they stick out their tongues and shake
    their heads.

[R] HEBREW TITLE: *A psalm by David.*

8 "You relied on the LORD," they say.
  "Why doesn't he save you?
If the LORD likes you,
  why doesn't he help you?"

9 It was you who brought me safely
     through birth,
  and when I was a baby, you kept me
     safe.
10 I have relied on you since the day I was
     born,
  and you have always been my God.
11 Do not stay away from me!
  Trouble is near,
  and there is no one to help.

12 Many enemies surround me like bulls;
  they are all around me,
  like fierce bulls from the land of
     Bashan.
13 They open their mouths like lions,
  roaring and tearing at me.

14 My strength is gone,
  gone like water spilled on the ground.
All my bones are out of joint;
  my heart is like melted wax.
15 My throat*h* is as dry as dust,
  and my tongue sticks to the roof of
     my mouth.
You have left me for dead in the dust.

16 A gang of evil men is around me;
  like a pack of dogs they close in on
     me;
  they tear at*i* my hands and feet.
17 All my bones can be seen.
  My enemies look at me and stare.
18 They gamble for my clothes
  and divide them among themselves.

---

h Probable text throat; *Hebrew* strength.   *i Some ancient translations*
they tear at; *others* they tie; *Hebrew* like a lion.

Come quickly to my rescue! (22.19)

¹⁹ O LORD, don't stay away from me!
    Come quickly to my rescue!
²⁰ Save me from the sword;
    save my life from these dogs.
²¹ Rescue me from these lions;
    I am helpless*ʲ* before these wild bulls.

²² I will tell my people what you have
      done;
    I will praise you in their assembly:
²³ "Praise him, you servants of the LORD!
    Honor him, you descendants of
      Jacob!
    Worship him, you people of Israel!
²⁴ He does not neglect the poor or ignore
      their suffering;
    he does not turn away from them,
    but answers when they call for help."

²⁵ In the full assembly I will praise you
      for what you have done;
    in the presence of those who worship
      you
    I will offer the sacrifices I promised.

ʲ Some ancient translations I am helpless; *Hebrew* you answered me.

²⁶ The poor will eat as much as they want;
 those who come to the LORD will
  praise him.
May they prosper forever!

²⁷ All nations will remember the LORD.
 From every part of the world they
  will turn to him;
 all races will worship him.
²⁸ The LORD is king,
 and he rules the nations.

²⁹ All proud men will bow down to him;ᵏ
 all mortal men will bow down before
  him.
³⁰ Future generations will serve him;
 men will speak of the Lord to the
  coming generation.
³¹ People not yet born will be told:
 "The LORD saved his people."

The LORD Our Shepherdˡ

23 The LORD is my shepherd;
  I have everything I need.
² He lets me rest in fields of green grass
 and leads me to quiet pools of fresh
  water.
³ He gives me new strength.
 He guides me in the right paths,
 as he has promised.
⁴ Even if I go through the deepest
  darkness,
 I will not be afraid, LORD,
 for you are with me.
Your shepherd's rod and staff protect
  me.

⁵ You prepare a banquet for me,
 where all my enemies can see me;

ᵏ *Probable text* will bow down to him; *Hebrew* will eat and bow
down. ˡ HEBREW TITLE: *A psalm by David.*

you welcome me as an honored guest
and fill my cup to the brim.
⁶ I know that your goodness and love
will be with me all my life;
and your house will be my home as
long as I live.

The Great King*m*

24   The world and all that is in it
belong to the LORD;
the earth and all who live on it are
his.
² He built it on the deep waters beneath
the earth
and laid its foundations in the ocean
depths.

³ Who has the right to go up the LORD's
hill?*n*
Who may enter his holy Temple?
⁴ Those who are pure in act and in
thought,
who do not worship idols
or make false promises.
⁵ The LORD will bless them and save
them;
God will declare them innocent.
⁶ Such are the people who come to God,
who come into the presence of the
God of Jacob.

⁷ Fling wide the gates,
open the ancient doors,
and the great king will come in.
⁸ Who is this great king?
He is the LORD, strong and mighty,
the LORD, victorious in battle.

---

m HEBREW TITLE: *A psalm by David.*   *n* THE LORD'S HILL: *The hill in
Jerusalem on which the Temple was built.*

⁹ Fling wide the gates,
    open the ancient doors,
    and the great king will come in.
¹⁰ Who is this great king?
  The triumphant LORD—he is the great
    king!

A Prayer for Guidance and Protection*

25 To you, O LORD, I offer my
        prayer;
²   in you, my God, I trust.
Save me from the shame of defeat;
    don't let my enemies gloat over me!
³ Defeat does not come to those who
    trust in you,
  but to those who are quick to rebel
    against you.

⁴ Teach me your ways, O LORD;
  make them known to me.
⁵ Teach me to live according to your
    truth,
  for you are my God, who saves me.
  I always trust in you.

⁶ Remember, O LORD, your kindness and
    constant love
  which you have shown from long
    ago.
⁷ Forgive the sins and errors of my
    youth.
In your constant love and goodness,
  remember me, LORD!

⁸ Because the LORD is righteous and
    good,
  he teaches sinners the path they
    should follow.
⁹ He leads the humble in the right way
  and teaches them his will.

º HEBREW TITLE: *By David.*

10 With faithfulness and love he leads
    all who keep his covenant and obey
    his commands.

11 Keep your promise, LORD, and forgive
    my sins,
    for they are many.
12 Those who obey the LORD
    will learn from him the path they
    should follow.
13 They will always be prosperous,
    and their children will possess the
    land.
14 The LORD is the friend of those who
    obey him
    and he affirms his covenant with
    them.

15 I look to the LORD for help at all times,
    and he rescues me from danger.
16 Turn to me, LORD, and be merciful to
    me,
    because I am lonely and weak.
17 Relieve me of my worries
    and save me from all my troubles.
18 Consider my distress and suffering
    and forgive all my sins.

19 See how many enemies I have;
    see how much they hate me.
20 Protect me and save me;
    keep me from defeat.
    I come to you for safety.
21 May my goodness and honesty preserve
    me,
    because I trust in you.

22 From all their troubles, O God,
    save your people Israel!

The Prayer of a Good Man[p]

26 Declare me innocent, O Lord,
      because I do what is right
and trust you completely.
2 Examine me and test me, Lord;
   judge my desires and thoughts.
3 Your constant love is my guide;
   your faithfulness always leads me.[q]

4 I do not keep company with worthless
      people;
   I have nothing to do with hypocrites.
5 I hate the company of evil men
   and avoid the wicked.

6 Lord, I wash my hands to show that I
      am innocent
   and march in worship around your
      altar.
7 I sing a hymn of thanksgiving
   and tell of all your wonderful deeds.

8 I love the house where you live, O
      Lord,
   the place where your glory dwells.
9 Do not destroy me with the sinners;
   spare me from the fate of
      murderers—
10 men who do evil all the time
   and are always ready to take bribes.

11 As for me, I do what is right;
   be merciful to me and save me!

12 I am safe from all dangers;
   in the assembly of his people I praise
      the Lord.

---

[p] HEBREW TITLE: By David.   [q] your faithfulness always leads me; or
I live in loyalty to you.

A Prayer of Praise[r]

27 The LORD is my light and my
salvation;
I will fear no one.
The LORD protects me from all danger;
I will never be afraid.

[2] When evil men attack me and try to kill
me,
they stumble and fall.
[3] Even if a whole army surrounds me,
I will not be afraid;
even if enemies attack me,
I will still trust God.[s]

[4] I have asked the LORD for one thing;
one thing only do I want:
to live in the LORD's house all my life,
to marvel there at his goodness,
and to ask for his guidance.
[5] In times of trouble he will shelter me;
he will keep me safe in his Temple
and make me secure on a high rock.
[6] So I will triumph over my enemies
around me.
With shouts of joy I will offer
sacrifices in his Temple;
I will sing, I will praise the LORD.

[7] Hear me, LORD, when I call to you!
Be merciful and answer me!
[8] When you said, "Come worship me,"
I answered, "I will come, LORD."
[9] Don't hide yourself from me!

Don't be angry with me;
don't turn your servant away.
You have been my help;
don't leave me, don't abandon me,
O God, my savior.

[r] HEBREW TITLE: *By David.*   [s] still trust God; *or* not lose courage.

10 My father and mother may abandon
    me,
  but the LORD will take care of me.

11 Teach me, LORD, what you want me to
    do,
  and lead me along a safe path,
  because I have many enemies.
12 Don't abandon me to my enemies,
  who attack me with lies and threats.

13 I know that I will live to see
  the LORD's goodness in this present
    life.
14 Trust in the LORD.
  Have faith, do not despair.
  Trust in the LORD.

A Prayer for Help[1]

28 O LORD, my defender, I call to
    you.
  Listen to my cry!
If you do not answer me,
  I will be among those who go down
  to the world of the dead.
2 Hear me when I cry to you for help,
  when I lift my hands toward your
    holy Temple.
3 Do not condemn me with the wicked,
  with those who do evil—
  men whose words are friendly,
  but who have hatred in their hearts.

4 Punish them for what they have done,
  for the evil they have committed.
  Punish them for all their deeds;
  give them what they deserve!

[1] HEBREW TITLE: *By David.*

⁵ They take no notice of what the LORD
      has done
   or of what he has made;
 so he will punish them
   and destroy them forever.

⁶ Give praise to the LORD;
   he has heard my cry for help.
⁷ The LORD protects and defends me;
   I trust in him.
 He gives me help and makes me glad;
   I praise him with joyful songs.

⁸ The LORD protects his people;
   he defends and saves his chosen king.
⁹ Save your people, LORD,
   and bless those who are yours.
 Be their shepherd,
   and take care of them forever.

The Voice of the LORD in the Stormᵘ

29 Praise the LORD, you heavenly
            beings;
   praise his glory and power.
² Praise the LORD's glorious name;
   bow down before the Holy One when
      he appears.ᵛ

³ The voice of the LORD is heard on the
      seas;
   the glorious God thunders,
   and his voice echoes over the ocean.
⁴ The voice of the LORD is heard
   in all its might and majesty.

⁵ The voice of the LORD breaks the
      cedars,
   even the cedars of Lebanon.

ᵘ HEBREW TITLE: *A psalm by David.* ᵛ when he appears; *or* in
garments of worship; *or* in his beautiful Temple.

⁶ He makes the mountains of Lebanon
  jump like calves
  and makes Mount Hermon leap like
  a young bull.

⁷ The voice of the LORD makes the
  lightning flash.
⁸ His voice makes the desert shake;
  he shakes the desert of Kadesh.
⁹ The LORD's voice shakes the oaks[w]
  and strips the leaves from the trees
  while everyone in his Temple shouts,
  "Glory to God!"

¹⁰ The LORD rules over the deep waters;
  he rules as king forever.
¹¹ The LORD gives strength to his people
  and blesses them with peace.

A Prayer of Thanksgiving[x]

30 I praise you, LORD, because you
     have saved me
  and kept my enemies from gloating
  over me.
² I cried to you for help, O LORD my
  God,
  and you healed me;
³   you kept me from the grave.
  I was on my way to the depths below,[y]
  but you restored my life.

⁴ Sing praise to the LORD,
  all his faithful people!
  Remember what the Holy One has
  done,
  and give him thanks!
⁵ His anger lasts only a moment,
  his goodness for a lifetime.
  Tears may flow in the night,
  but joy comes in the morning.

---

[w] *Probable text* shakes the oaks; *Hebrew* makes the deer give birth.
[x] HEBREW TITLE: *A song for the dedication of the Temple; a psalm by David.* [y] THE DEPTHS BELOW: *The world of the dead (see 6.5).*

⁶ I felt secure and said to myself,
  "I will never be defeated."
⁷ You were good to me, LORD;
    you protected me like a mountain
      fortress.
  But then you hid yourself from me,
    and I was afraid.

⁸ I called to you, LORD;
    I begged for your help:
⁹ "What will you gain from my death?
    What profit from my going to the
      grave?
  Are dead people able to praise you?
    Can they proclaim your unfailing
      goodness?
¹⁰ Hear me, LORD, and be merciful!
    Help me, LORD!"

¹¹ You have changed my sadness into a
      joyful dance;
    you have taken away my sorrow
    and surrounded me with joy.
¹² So I will not be silent;
    I will sing praise to you.
  LORD, you are my God;
    I will give you thanks forever.

A Prayer of Trust in God*

31 I come to you, LORD, for
         protection;
    never let me be defeated.
  You are a righteous God;
    save me, I pray!
² Hear me! Save me now!
  Be my refuge to protect me;
    my defense to save me.

³ You are my refuge and defense;
    guide me and lead me as you have
      promised.

---

* HEBREW TITLE: *A psalm by David.*

4 Keep me safe from the trap that has
       been set for me;
   shelter me from danger.
5 I place myself in your care.
   You will save me, LORD;
       you are a faithful God.

6 You hate those who worship false gods,
       but I trust in you.
7 I will be glad and rejoice
       because of your constant love.
   You see my suffering;
       you know my trouble.
8 You have not let my enemies capture
       me;
   you have given me freedom to go
       where I wish.

9 Be merciful to me, LORD,
       for I am in trouble;
   my eyes are tired from so much crying;
   I am completely worn out.
10 I am exhausted by sorrow,
       and weeping has shortened my life.
   I am weak from all my troubles;[a]
       even my bones are wasting away.

11 All my enemies, and especially my
       neighbors,
       treat me with contempt;
   Those who know me are afraid of me;
       when they see me in the street, they
       run away.
12 Everyone has forgotten me, as though I
       were dead;
   I am like something thrown away.
13 I hear many enemies whispering;
       terror is all around me.
   They are making plans against me,
       plotting to kill me.

[a] Some ancient translations troubles; Hebrew iniquity.

¹⁴ But my trust is in you, O LORD;
   you are my God.
¹⁵ I am always in your care;
   save me from my enemies,
   from those who persecute me.
¹⁶ Look on your servant with kindness;
   save me in your constant love.
¹⁷ I call to you, LORD;
   don't let me be disgraced.
 May the wicked be disgraced;
   may they go silently down to the
     world of the dead.
¹⁸ Silence those liars—
   all the proud and arrogant
   who speak with contempt about
     righteous men.

¹⁹ How wonderful are the good things
   you keep for those who honor you!
 Everyone knows how good you are,
   how securely you protect those who
     trust you.
²⁰ You hide them in the safety of your
     presence
   from the plots of men;
 in a safe shelter you hide them
   from the insults of their enemies.

²¹ Praise the LORD!
 How wonderfully he showed his love
     for me
   when I was surrounded and attacked!
²² I was afraid and thought
   that he had driven me out of his
     presence.
 But he heard my cry,
   when I called to him for help.

²³ Love the LORD, all his faithful people.
 The LORD protects the faithful,
   but punishes the proud as they
     deserve.

²⁴ Be strong, be courageous,
    all you that hope in the LORD.

Confession and Forgiveness[b]

32 Happy are those whose sins are
    forgiven,
    whose wrongs are pardoned.
² Happy is the man whom the LORD does
    not accuse of doing wrong
    and who is free from all deceit.

³ When I did not confess my sins,
    I was worn out from crying all day
      long.
⁴ Day and night you punished me, LORD;
    my strength was completely drained,
    as moisture is dried up by the
      summer heat.

⁵ Then I confessed my sins to you;
    I did not conceal my wrongdoings.
  I decided to confess them to you,
    and you forgave all my sins.

⁶ So all your loyal people should pray to
    you in times of need;[c]
    when a great flood of trouble comes
      rushing in,
    it will not reach them.
⁷ You are my hiding place;
    you will save me from trouble.
  I sing aloud of your salvation,
    because you protect me.

⁸ The LORD says, "I will teach you the
    way you should go;
    I will instruct you and advise you.

---

[b] HEBREW TITLE: *A poem by David.*   [c] *Some ancient translations*
need; *Hebrew* finding only.

⁹ Don't be stupid like a horse or a mule,
    which must be controlled with a bit
       and bridle
    to make it submit."

¹⁰ The wicked will have to suffer,
    but those who trust in the LORD
    are protected by his constant love.
¹¹ You that are righteous, be glad and
       rejoice
    because of what the LORD has done.
You that obey him, shout for joy!

A Song of Praise

33 All you that are righteous,
       shout for joy for what the LORD
       has done;
    praise him, all you that obey him.
² Give thanks to the LORD with harps,
    sing to him with stringed instruments.
³ Sing a new song to him,
    play the harp with skill, and shout for
       joy!

⁴ The words of the LORD are true,
    and all his works are dependable.
⁵ The LORD loves what is righteous and
       just;
    his constant love fills the earth.

⁶ The LORD created the heavens by his
       command,
    the sun, moon, and stars by his
       spoken word.
⁷ He gathered all the seas into one place;
    he shut up the ocean depths in
       storerooms.

⁸ Have reverence for the LORD, all the
       earth!
    Honor him, all peoples of the world!

⁹ When he spoke, the world was created;
    at his command everything appeared.

¹⁰ The LORD frustrates the purposes of the
      nations;
    he keeps them from carrying out their
      plans.
¹¹ But his plans endure forever;
    his purposes last eternally.
¹² Happy is the nation whose God is the
      LORD;
    happy are the people he has chosen
      for his own!

¹³ The LORD looks down from heaven
    and sees all mankind.
¹⁴ From where he rules, he looks down
    on all who live on earth.
¹⁵ He forms all their thoughts
    and knows everything they do.

¹⁶ A king does not win because of his
      powerful army;
    a soldier does not triumph because of
      his strength.
¹⁷ War horses are useless for victory;
    their great strength cannot save.

¹⁸ The LORD watches over those who have
      reverence for him,
    those who trust in his constant love.
¹⁹ He saves them from death;
    he keeps them alive in times of
      famine.

²⁰ We put our hope in the LORD;
    he is our protector and our help.
²¹ We are glad because of him;
    we trust in his holy name.

²² May your constant love be with us,
      LORD,
    as we put our hope in you.

In Praise of God's Goodness[d]

34 I will always thank the LORD;
　　　I will never stop praising him.
2 I will praise him for what he has done;
　　may all who are oppressed listen and
　　　be glad!
3 Proclaim with me the LORD's greatness;
　　let us praise his name together!

4 I prayed to the LORD, and he answered
　　me;
　　he freed me from all my fears.
5 The oppressed look to him and are
　　glad;
　　they will never be disappointed.
6 The helpless call to him, and he
　　answers;
　　he saves them from all their troubles.
7 His angel guards those who have
　　　reverence for the LORD
　　and rescues them from danger.

8 Find out for yourself how good the
　　LORD is.
　　Happy are those who find safety with
　　him.
9 Have reverence for the LORD, all his
　　people;
　　those who obey him have all they
　　need.
10 Even lions go hungry for lack of food,
　　but those who obey the LORD lack
　　nothing good.

11 Come, my young friends, and listen to
　　me,
　　and I will teach you to have
　　reverence for the LORD.
12 Would you like to enjoy life?
　　Do you want long life and happiness?

---

[d] HEBREW TITLE: *By David, who left the presence of Abimelech after
pretending to be crazy and being sent away by him.*

¹³ Then keep from speaking evil
and from telling lies.
¹⁴ Turn away from evil and do good;
strive for peace with all your heart.

¹⁵ The LORD watches over the righteous
and listens to their cries;
¹⁶ but he opposes those who do evil,
so that when they die, they are soon
forgotten.
¹⁷ The righteous call to the LORD, and he
listens;
he rescues them from all their
troubles.
¹⁸ The LORD is near to those who are
discouraged;
he saves those who have lost all
hope.

¹⁹ The good man suffers many troubles,
but the LORD saves him from them
all;
²⁰ the LORD preserves him completely;
not one of his bones is broken.
²¹ Evil will kill the wicked;
those who hate the righteous will be
punished.

²² The LORD will save his people;
those who go to him for protection
will be spared.

A Prayer for Help [c]

35 Oppose those who oppose me,
LORD,
and fight those who fight against me!
² Take your shield and armor
and come to my rescue.
³ Lift up your spear and war ax
against those who pursue me.
Promise that you will save me.

[c] HEBREW TITLE: *By David.*

⁴ May those who try to kill me
    be defeated and disgraced!
 May those who plot against me
    be turned back and confused!
⁵ May they be like straw blown by the
    wind
      as the angel of the LORD pursues
      them!
⁶ May their path be dark and slippery
      while the angel of the LORD strikes
      them down!

⁷ Without any reason they laid a trap for
    me
    and dug a deep hole to catch me.
⁸ But destruction will catch them before
      they know it;
      they will be caught in their own trap
      and fall to their destruction!

⁹ Then I will be glad because of the
      LORD;
    I will be happy because he saved me.
¹⁰ With all my heart I will say to the
      LORD,
    "There is no one like you.
    You protect the weak from the
      strong,
    the poor from the oppressor."

¹¹ Evil men testify against me
    and accuse me of crimes I know
      nothing about.
¹² They pay me back evil for good,
    and I sink in despair.
¹³ But when they were sick, I dressed in
      mourning;
    I deprived myself of food;
 I prayed with my head bowed low,
¹⁴   as I would pray for a friend or a
      brother.
 I went around bent over in mourning,
    as one who mourns for his mother.

¹⁵ But when I was in trouble, they were
    all glad
      and gathered around to make fun of
      me;
    strangers beat me
      and kept striking me.
¹⁶ Like men who would mock a cripple,ᶠ
    they glared at me with hate.

¹⁷ How much longer, Lord, will you just
    look on?
      Rescue me from their attacks;
      save my life from these lions!
¹⁸ Then I will thank you in the assembly
    of your people;
      I will praise you before them all.

¹⁹ Don't let my enemies, those liars,
    gloat over my defeat.
  Don't let those who hate me for no
    reason
      smirk with delight over my sorrow.

²⁰ They do not speak in a friendly way;
    instead they invent all kinds of lies
      about peace-loving people.
²¹ They accuse me, shouting,
    "We saw what you did!"
²² But you, O LORD, have seen this.
    So don't be silent, Lord;
      don't keep yourself far away!
²³ Rouse yourself, O Lord, and defend me;
    rise up, my God, and plead my cause.
²⁴ You are righteous, O LORD, so declare
    me innocent;
      don't let my enemies gloat over me.
²⁵ Don't let them say to themselves,
    "We are rid of him!
      That's just what we wanted!"

ᶠ Like . . . cripple; *Hebrew unclear.*

26 May those who gloat over my suffering
        be completely defeated and confused;
    may those who claim to be better than I
        am
        be covered with shame and disgrace.

27 May those who want to see me
        acquitted
        shout for joy and say again and again,
    "How great is the LORD!
        He is pleased with the success of his
        servant."
28 Then I will proclaim your
        righteousness,
    and I will praise you all day long.

The Wickedness of Man[g]

36 Sin speaks to the wicked man
        deep in his heart;
    he rejects God and does not have
        reverence for him.
2 Because he thinks so highly of himself,
    he thinks that God will not discover
        his sin and condemn it.
3 His speech is wicked and full of lies;
    he no longer does what is wise and
        good.
4 He makes evil plans as he lies in bed;
    nothing he does is good,
    and he never rejects anything evil.

The Goodness of God

5 LORD, your constant love reaches the
        heavens;
    your faithfulness extends to the skies.
6 Your righteousness is towering like the
        mountains;
    your justice is like the depths of the
        sea.
    Men and animals are in your care.

[g] HEBREW TITLE: *By David, the LORD's servant.*

⁷ How precious, O God, is your constant
    love!
    We find*ˣ* protection under the
       shadow of your wings.
⁸ We feast on the abundant food you
       provide;
    you let us drink from the river of
       your goodness.
⁹ You are the source of all life,
    and because of your light we see the
       light.

¹⁰ Continue to love those who know you
    and to do good to those who are
       righteous.
¹¹ Do not let proud men attack me
    or wicked men make me run away.

¹² See where evil men have fallen.
    There they lie, unable to rise.

The Destiny of the Wicked and of the Good*ʰ*

37 Don't be worried on account of
       the wicked;
    don't be jealous of those who do
       wrong.
² They will soon disappear like grass that
       dries up;
    they will die like plants that wither.

³ Trust in the LORD and do good;
    live in the land and be safe.
⁴ Seek your happiness in the LORD,
    and he will give you your heart's
       desire.

⁵ Give yourself to the LORD;
    trust in him, and he will help you;
⁶ he will make your righteousness shine
    like the noonday sun.

ˣ precious, O God, is . . . find; *or* precious is your constant love!
Gods and men find. *ʰ* HEBREW TITLE: *By David.*

7 Be patient and wait for the LORD to act;
    don't be worried about those who
      prosper
    or those who succeed in their evil
      plans.

8 Don't give in to worry or anger;
    it only leads to trouble.
9 Those who trust in the LORD will
      possess the land,
    but the wicked will be driven out.

10 Soon the wicked will disappear;
    you may look for them, but you
      won't find them;
11 but the humble will possess the land
    and enjoy prosperity and peace.

12 The wicked man plots against the good
      man
    and glares at him with hate.
13 But the Lord laughs at wicked men,
    because he knows they will soon be
      destroyed.

14 The wicked draw their swords and bend
      their bows
    to kill the poor and needy,
    to slaughter those who do what is
      right;
15 but they will be killed by their own
      swords,
    and their bows will be smashed.

16 The little that a good man owns
    is worth more than the wealth of all
      the wicked,
17 because the LORD will take away the
      strength of the wicked,
    but protect those who are good.

¹⁸ The LORD takes care of those who obey
       him,
    and the land will be theirs forever.
¹⁹ They will not suffer when times are
       bad;
    they will have enough in time of
       famine.
²⁰ But the wicked will die;
    the enemies of the LORD will vanish
       like wild flowers;
    they will disappear like smoke.

²¹ The wicked man borrows and never
       pays back,
    but the good man is generous with
       his gifts.
²² Those who are blessed by the LORD
       will possess the land,
    but those who are cursed by him will
       be driven out.

²³ The LORD guides a man in the way he
       should go
    and protects those who please him.
²⁴ If they fall, they will not stay down,
    because the LORD will help them up.

²⁵ I am an old man now; I have lived a
       long time,
    but I have never seen a good man
       abandoned by the LORD
    or his children begging for food.
²⁶ At all times he gives freely and lends to
       others,
    and his children are a blessing.

²⁷ Turn away from evil and do good,
    and your descendants will always live
       in the land;
²⁸ for the LORD loves what is right
    and does not abandon his faithful
       people.

He protects them forever,
    but the descendants of the wicked
      will be driven out.
29 The righteous will possess the land
    and live in it forever.

30 A good man's words are wise,
    and he is always fair.
31 He keeps the law of his God in his
      heart
    and never departs from it.

32 A wicked man watches a good man
    and tries to kill him;
33 but the LORD will not abandon him to
      his enemy's power
    or let him be condemned when he is
      on trial.

34 Put your hope in the LORD and obey
      his commands;
    he will honor you by giving you the
      land,
    and you will see the wicked driven
      out.

35 I once knew a wicked man who was a
      tyrant;
    he towered over everyone like a
      cedar of Lebanon;[i]
36 but later I[j] passed by, and he wasn't
      there;
    I looked for him, but couldn't find
      him.

37 Notice the good man, observe the
      righteous man;
    a peaceful man has descendants,
38 but sinners are completely destroyed,
    and their descendants are wiped out.

[i] *One ancient translation* like a cedar of Lebanon; *Hebrew unclear.*
[j] *Some ancient translations* I; *Hebrew* he.

³⁹ The LORD saves righteous men
    and protects them in times of trouble.
⁴⁰ He helps them and rescues them;
    he saves them from the wicked,
    because they go to him for protection.

The Prayer of a Suffering Man[k]

38 O LORD, don't punish me in your
    anger!
² You have wounded me with your
    arrows;
    you have struck me down.

³ Because of your anger, I am in great
    pain;
    my whole body is diseased because of
    my sins.
⁴ I am drowning in the flood of my sins;
    they are a burden too heavy to bear.

⁵ Because I have been foolish,
    my sores stink and rot.
⁶ I am bent over, I am crushed;
    I mourn all day long.
⁷ I am burning with fever
    and I am near death.
⁸ I am worn out and utterly crushed;
    my heart is troubled, and I groan
    with pain.

⁹ O Lord, you know what I long for;
    you hear all my groans.
¹⁰ My heart is pounding, my strength is
    gone,
    and my eyes have lost their
    brightness.
¹¹ My friends and neighbors will not come
    near me,
    because of my sores;
    even my family keeps away from me.

[k] HEBREW TITLE: *A psalm by David; a lament.*

¹² Those who want to kill me lay traps for
        me,
    and those who want to hurt me
        threaten to ruin me;
    they never stop plotting against me.

¹³ I am like a deaf man and cannot hear,
    like a dumb man and cannot speak.
¹⁴ I am like a man who does not answer,
    because he cannot hear.

¹⁵ But I trust in you, O Lord;
    and you, O Lord my God, will
        answer me.
¹⁶ Don't let my enemies gloat over my
        distress;
    don't let them boast about my
        downfall!
¹⁷ I am about to fall
    and am in constant pain.

¹⁸ I confess my sins;
    they fill me with anxiety.
¹⁹ My enemies are healthy and strong;
    there are many who hate me for no
        reason.
²⁰ Those who pay back evil for good
    are against me because I try to do
        right.

²¹ Do not abandon me, O Lord;
    do not stay away, my God!
²² Help me now, O Lord my savior!

The Confession of a Suffering Man[1]

39 I said, "I will be careful about
            what I do
    and will not let my tongue make me
        sin;
    I will not say anything
        while evil men are near."

[1] HEBREW TITLE: *A psalm by David.*

² I kept quiet, not saying a word,
    not even about anything good!
But my suffering only grew worse,
³ and I was overcome with anxiety.
The more I thought, the more troubled
      I became;
    I could not keep from asking:
⁴ "LORD, how long will I live?
    When will I die?
    Tell me how soon my life will end."

⁵ How short you have made my life!
    In your sight my lifetime seems
      nothing.
Indeed every living man is no more
      than a puff of wind,
⁶ no more than a shadow.
All he does is for nothing;
    he gathers wealth, but doesn't know
      who will get it.

⁷ What, then, can I hope for, Lord?
    I put my hope in you.
⁸ Save me from all my sins,
    and don't let fools make fun of me.
⁹ I will keep quiet, I will not say a word,
    for you are the one who made me
      suffer like this.
¹⁰ Don't punish me any more!
    I am about to die from your blows.
¹¹ You punish a man's sins by your
      rebukes,
    and like a moth you destroy what he
      loves.
Indeed a man is no more than a puff of
      wind!

¹² Hear my prayer, LORD,
    and listen to my cry;
    come to my aid when I weep.
Like all my ancestors
    I am only your guest for a little
      while.

¹³ Leave me alone so that I may have
   some happiness
 before I go away and am no more.

A Song of Praise [m]

40 I waited patiently for the LORD's
        help;
   then he listened to me and heard my
     cry.
² He pulled me out of a dangerous pit,
   out of the deadly quicksand.
 He set me safely on a rock
   and made me secure.
³ He taught me to sing a new song,
   a song of praise to our God.
 Many who see this will take warning
   and will put their trust in the LORD.

⁴ Happy are those who trust the LORD,
   who do not turn to idols
   or join those who worship false gods.
⁵ You have done many things for us, O
     LORD our God;
   there is no one like you!
 You have made many wonderful
     plans for us.
 I could never speak of them all—
   their number is so great!

⁶ You do not want sacrifices and
     offerings;
   you do not ask for animals burned
     whole on the altar
   or for sacrifices to take away sins.
 Instead, you have given me ears to hear
     you,
⁷   and so I answered, "Here I am;
   your instructions for me are in the
     book of the Law." [n]

[m] HEBREW TITLE: *A psalm by David.*   [n] your instructions . . . Law;
or my devotion to you is recorded in your book.

⁸ How I love to do your will, my God!
    I keep your teaching in my heart."

⁹ In the assembly of all your people,
      LORD,
    I told the good news that you save us.
    You know that I will never stop
      telling it.
¹⁰ I have not kept the news of salvation to
      myself;
    I have always spoken of your
      faithfulness and help.
In the assembly of all your people I
      have not been silent
about your loyalty and constant love.

¹¹ LORD, I know you will never stop being
      merciful to me.
    Your love and loyalty will always
      keep me safe.

A Prayer for Help
(Psalm 70)

¹² I am surrounded by many troubles—
    too many to count!
My sins have caught up with me,
    and I can no longer see;
they are more than the hairs of my
      head,
    and I have lost my courage.
¹³ Save me, LORD! Help me now!
¹⁴ May those who try to kill me
    be completely defeated and confused.
May those who are happy because of
      my troubles
    be turned back and disgraced.
¹⁵ May those who make fun of me
    be dismayed by their defeat.

¹⁶ May all who come to you
    be glad and joyful.

May all who are thankful for your
    salvation
    always say, "How great is the LORD!"

17 I am weak and poor, O Lord,
    but you have not forgotten me.
You are my savior and my God—
    hurry to my aid!

The Prayer of a Sick Man*o*

41 Happy are those who are
      concerned for the poor;
    the LORD will help them when they
      are in trouble.
2 The LORD will protect them and
      preserve their lives;
    he will make them happy in the land;
    he will not abandon them to the
      power of their enemies.
3 The LORD will help them when they
      are sick
    and will restore them to health.

4 I said, "I have sinned against you,
      LORD;
    be merciful to me and heal me."
5 My enemies say cruel things about me.
    They want me to die and be
      forgotten.
6 Those who come to see me are not
      sincere;
    they gather bad news about me
    and then go out and tell it
      everywhere.
7 All who hate me whisper to each other
      about me,
    they imagine the worst about*p* me.
8 They say, "He is fatally ill;
    he will never leave his bed again."

o HEBREW TITLE: *A psalm by David.*   *p* imagine the worst about; *or*
make evil plans to harm.

9 Even my best friend, the one I trusted
    most,
        the one who shared my food,
        has turned against me.

10 Be merciful to me, LORD, and restore
    my health,
        and I will pay my enemies back.
11 They will not triumph over me,
        and I will know that you are pleased
        with me.
12 You will help me, because I do what is
    right;
        you will keep me in your presence
        forever.

13 Praise the LORD, the God of Israel!
    Praise him now and forever!

Amen! Amen!

BOOK TWO
(Psalms 42—72)

The Prayer of a Man in Exile*q*

42 As a deer longs for a stream of
        cool water,
    so I long for you, O God.
2 I thirst for you, the living God.
    When can I go and worship in your
        presence?
3 Day and night I cry,
    and tears are my only food;
    all the time my enemies ask me,
        "Where is your God?"

---

q HEBREW TITLE: *A poem by the clan of Korah.*

⁴ My heart breaks when I remember the
    past,
   when I went with the crowds to the
       house of God
   and led them as they walked along,
   a happy crowd, singing and shouting
       praise to God.
⁵ Why am I so sad?
   Why am I so troubled?
  I will put my hope in God,
   and once again I will praise him,
   my savior and my God.

⁶⁻⁷ Here in exile my heart is breaking,
    and so I turn my thoughts to him.
   He has sent waves of sorrow over my
       soul;
    chaos roars at me like a flood,
    like waterfalls thundering down to
       the Jordan
    from Mount Hermon and Mount
       Mizar.
⁸ May the LORD show his constant love
    during the day,
   so that I may have a song at night,
   a prayer to the God of my life.

⁹ To God, my defender, I say,
   "Why have you forgotten me?
  Why must I go on suffering
   from the cruelty of my enemies?"
¹⁰ I am crushed by their insults,
   as they keep on asking me,
   "Where is your God?"

¹¹ Why am I so sad?
   Why am I so troubled?
  I will put my hope in God,
   and once again I will praise him,
   my savior and my God.

The Prayer of a Man in Exile
(Continuation of Psalm 42)

43 O God, declare me innocent,
    and defend my cause against
        the ungodly;
deliver me from lying and evil men!
2 You are my protector;
    why have you abandoned me?
Why must I go on suffering
    from the cruelty of my enemies?

3 Send your light and your truth;
    may they lead me
    and bring me back to Zion, your
        sacred hill,*r*
    and to your Temple, where you live.
4 Then I will go to your altar, O God;
    you are the source of my happiness.
I will play my harp and sing praise to
        you,
    O God, my God.

5 Why am I so sad?
    Why am I so troubled?
I will put my hope in God,
    and once again I will praise him,
    my savior and my God.

A Prayer for Protection*s*

44 With our own ears we have heard
    it, O God—
our ancestors have told us about it,
about the great things you did in their
        time,
    in the days of long ago:
2 how you yourself drove out the heathen
    and established your people in their
        land;
how you punished the other nations
    and caused your own to prosper.

---

r SACRED HILL: *See 2.6.*   *s* HEBREW TITLE: *A poem by the clan of Korah.*

3 Your people did not conquer the land
  with their swords;
    they did not win it by their own
    power;
  it was by your power and your strength,
    by the assurance of your presence,
    which showed that you loved them.

4 You are my king and my God;
    you give[t] victory to your people,
5   and by your power we defeat our
    enemies.
6 I do not trust in my bow
    or in my sword to save me;
7 but you have saved us from our
  enemies
    and defeated those who hate us.
8 We will always praise you
    and give thanks to you forever.

9 But now you have rejected us and let us
  be defeated;
    you no longer march out with our
    armies.
10 You made us run from our enemies,
    and they took for themselves what
    was ours.
11 You allowed us to be slaughtered like
  sheep;
    you scattered us in foreign countries.
12 You sold your own people for a small
  price
    as though they had little value.[u]

13 Our neighbors see what you did to us,
    and they mock us and laugh at us.
14 You have made us a joke among the
  nations;
    they shake their heads at us in scorn.

---

[t] *Some ancient translations* and my God; you give; *Hebrew* O God;
give.   [u] *as . . . value; or* and made no profit from the sale.

15 I am always in disgrace;
   I am covered with shame
16   from hearing the sneers and insults
      of my enemies and those who hate
         me.

17 All this has happened to us,
      even though we have not forgotten
         you
      or broken the covenant you made
         with us.
18 We have not been disloyal to you;
      we have not disobeyed your
         commands.
19 Yet you left us helpless among wild
         animals;
      you abandoned us in deepest
         darkness.

20 If we had stopped worshiping our God
      and prayed to a foreign god,
21 you would surely have discovered it,
      because you know our secret
         thoughts.
22 But it is on your account that we are
      being killed all the time,
      that we are treated like sheep to be
         slaughtered.

23 Wake up, Lord! Why are you asleep?
      Rouse yourself! Don't reject us
         forever!
24 Why are you hiding from us?
      Don't forget our suffering and
         trouble!

25 We fall crushed to the ground;
      we lie defeated in the dust.
26 Come to our aid!
      Because of your constant love save
         us!

A Royal Wedding Song[v]

45 Beautiful words fill my mind,
as I compose this song for the
king.
Like the pen of a good writer
my tongue is ready with a poem.

2 You are the most handsome of men;
you are an eloquent speaker.
God has always blessed you.
3 Buckle on your sword, mighty king;
you are glorious and majestic.

4 Ride on in majesty to victory
for the defense of truth and justice![w]
Your strength will win you great
victories!
5 Your arrows are sharp,
they pierce the hearts of your
enemies;
nations fall down at your feet.

6 The kingdom that God has given you[x]
will last forever and ever.
You rule over your people with justice;
7 you love what is right and hate what
is evil.
That is why God, your God, has chosen
you
and has poured out more happiness
on you
than on any other king.
8 The perfume of myrrh and aloes is on
your clothes;
musicians entertain you in palaces
decorated with ivory.

[v] HEBREW TITLE: *A poem by the clan of Korah; a love song.*
[w] *Probable text* and justice; *Hebrew* and meekness of justice. [x] The
kingdom that God has given you; *or* Your kingdom, O God; *or*
Your divine kingdom.

⁹ Among the ladies of your court are
    daughters of kings,
      and at the right of your throne stands
      the queen,
      wearing ornaments of finest gold.

¹⁰ Bride of the king, listen to what I say—
    forget your people and your relatives.
¹¹ Your beauty will make the king desire
    you;
      he is your master, so you must obey
      him.
¹² The people of Tyre will bring you gifts;
    rich people will try to win your favor.

¹³ The princess is in the palace—how
    beautiful she is!
      Her gown is made of gold thread.
¹⁴ In her colorful gown she is led to the
    king,
      followed by her bridesmaids,
      and they also are brought to him.
¹⁵ With joy and gladness they come
    and enter the king's palace.

¹⁶ You, my king, will have many sons
    to succeed your ancestors as kings,
      and you will make them rulers over
      the whole earth.
¹⁷ My song will keep your fame alive
    forever,
      and everyone will praise you for all
      time to come.

God Is with Us^y

46 God is our shelter and strength,
    always ready to help in times of
    trouble.

^y HEBREW TITLE: *A song by the clan of Korah.*

We will not be afraid. (46.2)

2 So we will not be afraid, even if the
    earth is shaken
      and mountains fall into the ocean
        depths;
3 even if the seas roar and rage,
      and the hills are shaken by the
        violence.

4 There is a river that brings joy to the
      city of God,
      to the sacred house of the Most High.
5 God is in that city, and it will never be
      destroyed;
      at early dawn he will come to its aid.
6 Nations are terrified, kingdoms are
      shaken;
      God thunders, and the earth
        dissolves.

7 The LORD Almighty is with us;
      the God of Jacob is our refuge.

⁸ Come and see what the LORD has done.
   See what amazing things he has done
      on earth.
⁹ He stops wars all over the world;
   he breaks bows, destroys spears,
      and sets shields on fire.
¹⁰ "Stop fighting," he says, "and know that
      I am God,
   supreme among the nations,
   supreme over the world."

¹¹ The LORD Almighty is with us;
   the God of Jacob is our refuge.

Sing praise to God. (47.6)

The Supreme Ruler[z]

47 Clap your hands for joy, all
      peoples!
   Praise God with loud songs!
² The LORD, the Most High, is to be
      feared;
   he is a great king, ruling over all the
      world.

[z] HEBREW TITLE: *A psalm by the clan of Korah.*

³ He gave us victory over the peoples;
   he made us rule over the nations.
⁴ He chose for us the land where we live,
   the proud possession of his people,
      whom he loves.

⁵ God goes up to his throne.
      There are shouts of joy and the blast
         of trumpets,
      as the LORD goes up.
⁶ Sing praise to God;
      sing praise to our king!
⁷ God is king over all the world;
      praise him with songs!

⁸ God sits on his sacred throne;
      he rules over the nations.
⁹ The rulers of the nations assemble
      with the people*a* of the God of
         Abraham.
   More powerful than all armies is he;
      he rules supreme.

Zion, the City of God*b*

48   The LORD is great and is to be
        highly praised
   in the city of our God, on his sacred
      hill.*c*
² Zion, the mountain of God, is high and
      beautiful;
      the city of the great king brings joy to
         all the world.
³ God has shown that there is safety with
      him
   inside the fortresses of the city.

⁴ The kings gathered together
      and came to attack Mount Zion.

a Probable text with the people; *Hebrew* the people.   *b* HEBREW
TITLE: *A psalm by the clan of Korah; a song.*   *c* SACRED HILL: *See*
2.6.

⁵ But when they saw it, they were
     amazed;
  they were afraid and ran away.
⁶ There they were seized with fear and
     anguish,
  like a woman about to bear a child,
⁷   like ships tossing in a furious storm.

⁸ We have heard what God has done,
     and now we have seen it
  in the city of our God, the LORD
     Almighty;
  he will keep the city safe forever.

⁹ Inside your Temple, O God,
  we think of your constant love.
¹⁰ You are praised by people everywhere,
     and your fame extends over all the
     earth.
  You rule with justice;
¹¹   let the people of Zion be glad!
  You give right judgments;
     let there be joy in the cities of Judah!

¹² People of God, walk around Zion and
     count the towers;
¹³   take notice of the walls and examine
     the fortresses,
  so that you may tell the next
     generation:
¹⁴   "This God is our God forever and
     ever;
  he will lead us for all time to come."

The Foolishness of Trusting in Riches[d]

49 Hear this, everyone!
     Listen, all people everywhere,
²   great and small alike,
  rich and poor together.

[d] HEBREW TITLE: *A psalm by the clan of Korah.*

³ My thoughts will be clear;
    I will speak words of wisdom.
⁴ I will turn my attention to proverbs
    and explain their meaning as I play
       the harp.

⁵ I am not afraid in times of danger
    when I am surrounded by enemies,
⁶ by evil men who trust in their riches
    and boast of their great wealth.
⁷ A person can never redeem himself;
    he cannot pay God the price for his
       life,
⁸   because the payment for a human life
    is too great.
What he could pay would never be
    enough
⁹   to keep him from the grave,
    to let him live forever.

¹⁰ Anyone can see that even wise men die,
    as well as foolish and stupid men.
    They all leave their riches to their
       descendants.
¹¹ Their graves*ᵉ* are their homes forever;
    there they stay for all time,
    though they once had lands of their
       own.
¹² A man's greatness cannot keep him
    from death;
    he will still die like the animals.

¹³ See what happens to those who trust in
    themselves,
    the fate of those*ᶠ* who are satisfied
       with their wealth—
¹⁴ they are doomed to die like sheep,
    and Death will be their shepherd.

ᵉ Some ancient translations graves; *Hebrew* inner thoughts. *ᶠ One*
ancient translation the fate of those; *Hebrew* after them.

The righteous will triumph over them,
   as their bodies quickly decay
   in the world of the dead far from
      their homes.[g]
15 But God will rescue me;
   he will save me from the power of
      death.

16 Don't be upset when a man becomes
      rich,
   when his wealth grows even greater;
17 he cannot take it with him when he
      dies;
   his wealth will not go with him to the
      grave.
18 Even if a man is satisfied with this life
   and is praised because he is
      successful,
19 he will join all his ancestors in death,
   where the darkness lasts forever.
20 A man's greatness cannot keep him
      from death;
   he will still die like the animals.

True Worship[h]

50 The Almighty God, the LORD,
      speaks;
   he calls to the whole earth from east
      to west.
2 God shines from Zion,
   the city perfect in its beauty.

3 Our God is coming, but not in silence;
   a raging fire is in front of him,
   a furious storm around him.
4 He calls heaven and earth as witnesses
   to see him judge his people.

[g] in . . . homes.; *Hebrew unclear.*   [h] HEBREW TITLE: *A psalm by Asaph.*

5 He says, "Gather my faithful people to
    me,
        those who made a covenant with me
        by offering a sacrifice."
6 The heavens proclaim that God is
        righteous,
        that he himself is judge.

7 "Listen, my people, and I will speak;
        I will testify against you, Israel.
        I am God, your God.
8 I do not reprimand you because of your
        sacrifices
        and the burnt offerings you always
        bring me.
9 And yet I do not need bulls from your
        farms
        or goats from your flocks;
10 all the animals in the forest are mine
        and the cattle on thousands of hills.
11 All the wild birds are mine
        and all living things in the fields.

12 "If I were hungry, I would not ask you
        for food,
        for the world and everything in it is
        mine.
13 Do I eat the flesh of bulls
        or drink the blood of goats?
14 Let the giving of thanks be your
        sacrifice to God,[i]
        and give the Almighty all that you
        promised.
15 Call to me when trouble comes;
        I will save you,
        and you will praise me."

16 But God says to the wicked,
        "Why should you recite my
        commandments?
        Why should you talk about my
        covenant?

[i] Let the giving . . . to God; *or* Offer your thanksgiving sacrifice to
God.

The animals in the forest are mine. (50.10)

¹⁷ You refuse to let me correct you;
 you reject my commands.
¹⁸ You become the friend of every thief
  you see,
 and you associate with adulterers.

¹⁹ "You are always ready to speak evil;
 you never hesitate to tell lies.
²⁰ You are ready to accuse your own
  brothers
 and to find fault with them.
²¹ You have done all this, and I have said
  nothing,
 so you thought that I am like you.
But now I reprimand you
 and make the matter plain to you.

²² "Listen to this, you that ignore me,
 or I will destroy you,
 and there will be no one to save you.
²³ Giving thanks is the sacrifice that
  honors me,
 and I will surely save all who obey
  me."

A Prayer for Forgiveness ^j

51   Be merciful to me, O God,
   because of your constant love.
Because of your great mercy
 wipe away my sins!
² Wash away all my evil
 and make me clean from my sin!

³ I recognize my faults;
 I am always conscious of my sins.
⁴ I have sinned against you—only against
  you—
 and done what you consider evil.
So you are right in judging me;
 you are justified in condemning me.

^j HEBREW TITLE: *A psalm by David, after the prophet Nathan had spoken to him about his adultery with Bathsheba.*

⁵ I have been evil from the day I was
    born;
  from the time I was conceived, I have
    been sinful.

⁶ Sincerity and truth are what you
    require;
  fill my mind with your wisdom.
⁷ Remove my sin, and I will be clean;
  wash me, and I will be whiter than
    snow.
⁸ Let me hear the sounds of joy and
    gladness;
  and though you have crushed me and
    broken me,
  I will be happy once again.
⁹ Close your eyes to my sins
  and wipe out all my evil.

¹⁰ Create a pure heart in me, O God,
  and put a new and loyal spirit in me.
¹¹ Do not banish me from your presence;
  do not take your holy spirit away
    from me.
¹² Give me again the joy that comes from
    your salvation,
  and make me willing to obey you.
¹³ Then I will teach sinners your
    commands,
  and they will turn back to you.

¹⁴ Spare my life, O God, and save me,ᵏ
  and I will gladly proclaim your
    righteousness.
¹⁵ Help me to speak, Lord,
  and I will praise you.

¹⁶ You do not want sacrifices,
  or I would offer them;
  you are not pleased with burnt
    offerings.

ᵏ Spare my life . . . me; or O God my savior, keep me from the
crime of murder.

¹⁷ My sacrifice is a humble spirit, O God;
    you will not reject a humble and
        repentant heart.

¹⁸ O God, be kind to Zion and help her;
    rebuild the walls of Jerusalem.
¹⁹ Then you will be pleased with proper
        sacrifices
    and with our burnt offerings;
    and bulls will be sacrificed on your
        altar.

God's Judgment and Grace *

52 Why do you boast, great man, of
        your evil?
    God's faithfulness is eternal.
² You make plans to ruin others;
    your tongue is like a sharp razor.
    You are always inventing lies.
³ You love evil more than good
    and falsehood more than truth.
⁴ You love to hurt people with your
        words, you liar!

⁵ So God will ruin you forever;
    he will take hold of you and snatch
        you from your home;
    he will remove you from the world of
        the living.
⁶ Righteous people will see this and be
        afraid;
    Then they will laugh at you and say,
⁷ "Look, here is a man who did not
        depend on God for safety,
    but trusted instead in his great wealth
    and looked for security in being
        wicked."

---

* HEBREW TITLE: *A poem by David, after Doeg the Edomite went to Saul and told him that David had gone to the house of Ahimelech.*

⁸ But I am like an olive tree growing in
the house of God;
I trust in his constant love forever
and ever.
⁹ I will always thank you, God, for what
you have done;
in the presence of your people
I will proclaim that you are good.

The Wickedness of Men ᵐ

(Psalm 14)

53 Fools say to themselves,
"There is no God."
They are all corrupt,
and they have done terrible things;
there is no one who does what is
right.

² God looks down from heaven at
mankind
to see if there are any who are wise,
any who worship him.
³ But they have all turned away;
they are all equally bad.
Not one of them does what is right,
not a single one.

⁴ "Don't they know?" God asks.
"Are these evildoers ignorant?
They live by robbing my people,
and they never pray to me."

⁵ But then they will become terrified,
as they have never been before,
for God will scatter the bones of the
enemies of his people.
God has rejected them,
and so Israel will totally defeat them.

ᵐ HEBREW TITLE: *A poem by David.*

[6] How I pray that victory
will come to Israel from Zion.
How happy the people of Israel will be
when God makes them prosperous
again!

A Prayer for Protection from Enemies[n]

54 Save me by your power, O God;
set me free by your might!
[2] Hear my prayer, O God;
listen to my words!
[3] Proud men are coming to attack me;
cruel men are trying to kill me—
men who do not care about God.

[4] But God is my helper.
The Lord is my defender.
[5] May God use their own evil to punish
my enemies.
He will destroy them because he is
faithful.

[6] I will gladly offer you a sacrifice, O
LORD;
I will give you thanks
because you are good.
[7] You have rescued me from all my
troubles,
and I have seen my enemies defeated.

The Prayer of a Man Betrayed by a Friend[o]

55 Hear my prayer, O God;
don't turn away from my plea!
[2] Listen to me and answer me;
I am worn out by my worries.

[n] HEBREW TITLE: *A poem by David, after the men from Ziph went to
Saul and told him that David was hiding in their territory.* [o] HEBREW
TITLE: *A poem by David.*

I wish I had wings like a dove. (55.6)

³ I am terrified by the threats of my
  enemies,
    crushed by the oppression of the
    wicked.
They bring trouble on me;
    they are angry with me and hate me.

⁴ I am terrified,
    and the terrors of death crush me.
⁵ I am gripped by fear and trembling;
    I am overcome with horror.
⁶ I wish I had wings like a dove.
    I would fly away and find rest.
⁷ I would fly far away
    and live in the wilderness.
⁸ I would hurry and find myself a shelter
    from the raging wind and the storm.
⁹ Confuse the speech of my enemies, O
    Lord!

I see violence and riots in the city,
10   surrounding it day and night,
    filling it with crime and trouble.

11 There is destruction everywhere;
      the streets are full of oppression and
          fraud.

12 If it were an enemy making fun of me,
      I could endure it;
   if it were an opponent boasting over
          me,
      I could hide myself from him.
13 But it is you, my companion,
      my colleague and close friend.
14 We had intimate talks with each other
      and worshiped together in the
          Temple.
15 May my enemies die before their time;
      may they go down alive into the
          world of the dead!
   Evil is in their homes and in their
          hearts.

16 But I call to the LORD God for help,
      and he will save me.
17 Morning, noon, and night
      my complaints and groans go up to
          him,
      and he will hear my voice.
18 He will bring me safely back
      from the battles that I fight
          against so many enemies.
19 God, who has ruled from eternity,
      will hear me and defeat them;
   for they refuse to change,
      and they do not fear him.

20 My former companion attacked his
          friends;
      he broke his promises.
21 His words were smoother than cream,
      but there was hatred in his heart;
   his words were as soothing as oil,
      but they cut like sharp swords.

²² Leave your troubles with the LORD,
    and he will defend you;
    he never lets honest men be defeated.

²³ But you, O God, will bring those
        murderers and liars to their graves
    before half their life is over.
    As for me, I will trust in you.

A Prayer of Trust in God^p

56 Be merciful to me, O God,
        because I am under attack;
    my enemies persecute me all the
        time.
² All day long my opponents attack me.
    There are so many who fight against
        me.
³ When I am afraid, O LORD Almighty,
    I put my trust in you.
⁴ I trust in God and am not afraid;
    I praise him for what he has
        promised.
    What can a mere human being do to
        me?

⁵ My enemies make trouble for me all
        day long;
    they are always thinking up some
        way to hurt me!
⁶ They gather in hiding places
    and watch everything I do,
    hoping to kill me.
⁷ Punish^q them, O God, for their evil;
    defeat those people in your anger!

⁸ You know how troubled I am;
    you have kept a record of my tears.
    Aren't they listed in your book?

---

^p HEBREW TITLE: *A psalm by David, after the Philistines captured him in Gath.* ^q *Probable text* Punish; *Hebrew* Save.

⁹ The day I call to you,
    my enemies will be turned back.
I know this: God* is on my side—
¹⁰   the LORD, whose promises I praise.
¹¹ In him I trust, and I will not be afraid.
    What can a mere human being do to
      me?

¹² O God, I will offer you what I have
    promised;
    I will give you my offering of
      thanksgiving,
¹³ because you have rescued me from
    death
    and kept me from defeat.
And so I walk in the presence of God,
    in the light that shines on the living.

A Prayer for Help*

57 Be merciful to me, O God, be
        merciful,
because I come to you for safety.
In the shadow of your wings I find
    protection
    until the raging storms are over.

² I call to God, the Most High,
    to God, who supplies my every need.
³ He will answer from heaven and save
    me;
    he will defeat my oppressors.
God will show me his constant love
    and faithfulness.

⁴ I am surrounded by enemies,
    who are like man-eating lions.
Their teeth are like spears and arrows;
    their tongues are like sharp swords.

I know this: God; or Because I know that God.   *HEBREW TITLE:
A psalm by David, after he fled from Saul in the cave.*

⁵ Show your greatness in the sky, O God,
    and your glory over all the earth.

⁶ My enemies have spread a net to catch
    me;
    I am overcome with distress.
  They dug a pit in my path,
    but fell into it themselves.

⁷ I have complete confidence, O God;
    I will sing and praise you!
⁸ Wake up, my soul!
    Wake up, my harp and lyre!
    I will wake up the sun.
⁹ I will thank you, O Lord, among the
    nations.
    I will praise you among the peoples.
¹⁰ Your constant love reaches the heavens;
    your faithfulness touches the skies.
¹¹ Show your greatness in the sky, O God,
    and your glory over all the earth.

A Prayer for God to Punish the Wicked[t]

58   Do you rulers[u] ever give a just
      decision?
   Do you judge all men fairly?
² No! You think only of the evil you can
    do,
    and commit crimes of violence in the
    land.

³ Evil men go wrong all their lives;
    they tell lies from the day they are
    born.
⁴ They are full of poison like snakes;
    they stop up their ears like a deaf
    cobra,
⁵ which does not hear the voice of the
    snake charmer,
    or the chant of the clever magician.

---

[t] HEBREW TITLE: *A psalm by David.* [u] rulers; *or* gods.

6 Break the teeth of these fierce lions, O
    God.
7 May they disappear like water draining
    away;
    may they be crushed like weeds on a
    path.ᵛ
8 May they be like snails that dissolve
    into slime;
    may they be like a baby born dead
    that never sees the light.
9 Before they know it, they are cut down
    like weeds;
    in his fierce anger God will blow
    them away
    while they are still living.ʷ

10 The righteous will be glad when they
    see sinners punished;
    they will wade through the blood of
    the wicked.
11 People will say, "The righteous are
    indeed rewarded;
    there is indeed a God who judges the
    world."

A Prayer for Safetyˣ

59 Save me from my enemies, my
        God;
    protect me from those who attack me!
2 Save me from those evil men;
    rescue me from those murderers!

3 Look! They are waiting to kill me;
    cruel men are gathering against me.
    It is not because of any sin or wrong I
    have done,
4   nor because of any fault of mine, O
    LORD,
    that they hurry to their places.

ᵛ Probable text may . . . path; Hebrew unclear. ʷ Verse 9 in Hebrew
is unclear. ˣ HEBREW TITLE: A psalm by David, after Saul sent men
to watch his house in order to kill him.

⁵ Rise, LORD God Almighty, and come to
      my aid;
   see for yourself, God of Israel!
Wake up and punish the heathen;
   show no mercy to evil traitors!

⁶ They come back in the evening,
      snarling like dogs as they go about
      the city.
⁷ Listen to their insults and threats.
Their tongues are like swords in their
      mouths,
   yet they think that no one hears
      them.

⁸ But you laugh at them, LORD;
   you mock all the heathen.
⁹ I have confidence in your strength;
   you are my refuge, O God.
¹⁰ My God loves me and will come to me;
   he will let me see my enemies
      defeated.

¹¹ Do not kill them, O God, or my people
      may forget.
   Scatter them by your strength and
      defeat them,
   O Lord, our protector.
¹² Sin is on their lips; all their words are
      sinful;
   may they be caught in their pride!
Because they curse and lie,
¹³   destroy them in your anger;
   destroy them completely.
Then everyone will know that God
      rules in Israel,
   that his rule extends over all the
      earth.

¹⁴ My enemies come back in the evening,
      snarling like dogs as they go about
      the city,

15   like dogs roaming about for food
      and growling if they do not find
          enough.

16 But I will sing about your strength;
       every morning I will sing aloud of
          your constant love.
   You have been a refuge for me,
       a shelter in my time of trouble.
17 I will praise you, my defender.
       My refuge is God,
          the God who loves me.

A Prayer for Deliverance[y]

60   You have rejected us, God, and
          defeated us;
       you have been angry with us—but
          now turn back to us.[z]
2 You have made the land tremble, and
          you have cut it open;
       now heal its wounds, because it is
          falling apart.
3 You have made your people suffer
          greatly;
       we stagger around as though we were
          drunk.
4 You have warned those who have
          reverence for you,
       so that they might escape
          destruction.
5 Save us by your might; answer our
          prayer,
       so that the people you love may be
          rescued.

[y] HEBREW TITLE: *A psalm by David, for teaching, when he fought
against the Arameans from Naharaim and from Zobah, and Joab
turned back and killed 12,000 Edomites in Salt Valley.*   [z] *angry with
us . . . us; or angry with us and turned your back on us.*

⁶ From his sanctuary*a* God has said,
   "In triumph I will divide Shechem
   and distribute Sukkoth Valley to my
     people.
⁷ Gilead is mine, and Manasseh too;
   Ephraim is my helmet
   and Judah my royal scepter.
⁸ But I will use Moab as my washbowl,
   and I will throw my sandals on
     Edom,
   as a sign that I own it.
   Did the Philistines think they would
     shout in triumph over me?"

⁹ Who, O God, will take me into the
     fortified city?
   Who will lead me to Edom?
¹⁰ Have you really rejected us?
   Aren't you going to march out with
     our armies?
¹¹ Help us against the enemy;
   human help is worthless.
¹² With God on our side we will win;
   he will defeat our enemies.

A Prayer for Protection*b*

61   Hear my cry, O God;
       listen to my prayer!
² In despair and far from home
   I call to you!

   Take me to a safe refuge,
³   for you are my protector,
   my strong defense against my
     enemies.

⁴ Let me live in your sanctuary all my
     life;
   let me find safety under your wings.

---

a From his sanctuary; *or* In his holiness.   *b* HEBREW TITLE: *By David.*

Take me to a safe refuge. (61.2)

⁵ You have heard my promises, O God,
   and you have given me what belongs
      to those who honor you.

⁶ Add many years to the king's life;
   let him live on and on!
⁷ May he rule forever in your presence,
      O God;
   protect him with your constant love
      and faithfulness.

⁸ So I will always sing praises to you,
   as I offer you daily what I have
      promised.

Confidence in God's Protection*

62 I wait patiently for God to save
   me;
   I depend on him alone.

* HEBREW TITLE: *A psalm by David.*

² He alone protects and saves me;
    he is my defender,
    and I shall never be defeated.

³ How much longer will all of you attack
    a man
    who is no stronger than a broken-
    down fence?
⁴ You only want to bring him down from
    his place of honor;
    you take pleasure in lies.
You speak words of blessing,
    but in your heart you curse him.

⁵ I depend on God alone;
    I put my hope in him.
⁶ He alone protects and saves me;
    he is my defender,
    and I shall never be defeated.
⁷ My salvation and honor depend on
    God;
    he is my strong protector;
    he is my shelter.

⁸ Trust in God at all times, my people.
    Tell him all your troubles,
    for he is our refuge.

⁹ Men are all like a puff of breath;
    great and small alike are worthless.
Put them on the scales, and they weigh
    nothing;
    they are lighter than a mere breath.
¹⁰ Don't put your trust in violence;
    don't hope to gain anything by
    robbery;
even if your riches increase,
    don't depend on them.

¹¹ More than once I have heard God say
    that power belongs to him
¹²   and that his love is constant.
You yourself, O Lord, reward everyone
    according to his deeds.

Longing for God[d]

63 O God, you are my God,
and I long for you.
My whole being desires you;
like a dry, worn-out, and waterless
land,
my soul is thirsty for you.
2 Let me see you in the sanctuary;
let me see how mighty and glorious
you are.
3 Your constant love is better than life
itself,
and so I will praise you.
4 I will give you thanks as long as I live;
I will raise my hands to you in
prayer.
5 My soul will feast and be satisfied,
and I will sing glad songs of praise to
you.

6 As I lie in bed, I remember you;
all night long I think of you,
7 because you have always been my
help.
In the shadow of your wings I sing for
joy.
8 I cling to you,
and your hand keeps me safe.

9 Those who are trying to kill me
will go down into the world of the
dead.
10 They will be killed in battle,
and their bodies eaten by wolves.
11 Because God gives him victory,
the king will rejoice.
Those who make promises in God's
name will praise him,
but the mouths of liars will be shut.

[d] HEBREW TITLE: *A psalm by David, when he was in the desert of
Judea.*

A Prayer for Protection[e]

64 I am in trouble, God—listen to
my prayer!
I am afraid of my enemies—save my
life!

2 Protect me from the plots of the
wicked,
from mobs of evil men.
3 They sharpen their tongues like swords
and aim cruel words like arrows.
4 They are quick to spread their
shameless lies;
they destroy good men with cowardly
slander.
5 They encourage each other in their evil
plots;
they talk about where they will place
their traps.
"No one can see them," they say.
6 They make evil plans and say,
"We have planned a perfect crime."
The heart and mind of man are a
mystery.

7 But God shoots his arrows at them,
and suddenly they are wounded.
8 He will destroy them because of those
words;[f]
all who see them will shake their
heads.
9 They will all be afraid;
they will think about what God has
done
and tell about his deeds.
10 All righteous people will rejoice
because of what the LORD has done.
They will find safety in him;
all good people will praise him.

[e] HEBREW TITLE: *A psalm by David.* [f] *Probable text* He will destroy
them because of those words; *Hebrew* They will destroy him, those
words are against them.

Praise and Thanksgiving[g]

65 O God, it is right for us to praise
        you in Zion
    and keep our promises to you,
2   because you answer prayers.
    People everywhere will come to you
3   on account of their sins.
    Our faults defeat us,[h]
        but you forgive them.
4 Happy are those whom you choose,
        whom you bring to live in your
            sanctuary.
    We shall be satisfied with the good
        things of your house,
        the blessings of your sacred Temple.

5 You answer us by giving us victory,
        and you do wonderful things to save
            us.
    People all over the world
        and across the distant seas trust in
            you.
6 You set the mountains in place by your
        strength,
        showing your mighty power.
7 You calm the roar of the seas
        and the noise of the waves;
        you calm the uproar of the peoples.
8 The whole world stands in awe
        of the great things that you have
            done.
    Your deeds bring shouts of joy
        from one end of the earth to the
            other.

9 You show your care for the land by
        sending rain;
        you make it rich and fertile.

[g] HEBREW TITLE: *A psalm by David; a song.*   [h] *One ancient
translation* us; *Hebrew* me.

You fill the streams with water;
    you provide the earth with crops.
This is how you do it:
¹⁰   you send abundant rain on the
      plowed fields
    and soak them with water;
you soften the soil with showers
    and cause the young plants to grow.
¹¹ What a rich harvest your goodness
      provides!
    Wherever you go there is plenty.
¹² The pastures are filled with flocks;
    the hillsides are full of joy.
¹³ The fields are covered with sheep;
    the valleys are full of wheat.
Everything shouts and sings for joy.

A Song of Praise and Thanksgiving*i*

66 Praise God with shouts of joy, all
people!
² Sing to the glory of his name;
    offer him glorious praise!
³ Say to God, "How wonderful are the
      things you do!
    Your power is so great
    that your enemies bow down in fear
      before you.
⁴ Everyone on earth worships you;
    they sing praises to you,
    they sing praises to your name."

⁵ Come and see what God has done,
    his wonderful acts among men.
⁶ He changed the sea into dry land;
    our ancestors crossed the river on
      foot.
There we rejoiced because of what he
      did.
⁷ He rules forever by his might
    and keeps his eyes on the nations.
    Let no rebels rise against him.

i HEBREW TITLE: *A song.*

Sing to the glory of his name. (66.2)

8 Praise our God, all nations;
   let your praise be heard.
9 He has kept us alive
   and has not allowed us to fall.

10 You have put us to the test, God;
   as silver is purified by fire,
   so you have tested us.
11 You let us fall into a trap
   and placed heavy burdens on our
      backs.
12 You let our enemies trample us;
   we went through fire and flood,
   but now you have brought us to a
      place of safety.*j*

13 I will bring burnt offerings to your
      house;
   I will offer you what I promised.
14 I will give you what I said I would
   when I was in trouble.
15 I will offer sheep to be burned on the
      altar;
   I will sacrifice bulls and goats,
   and the smoke will go up to the sky.

16 Come and listen, all who honor God,
   and I will tell you what he has done
      for me.

j Some ancient translations safety; *Hebrew* overflowing.

¹⁷ I cried to him for help;
    I praised him with songs.
¹⁸ If I had ignored my sins,
    the Lord would not have listened to
        me.
¹⁹ But God has indeed heard me;
    he has listened to my prayer.

²⁰ I praise God,
    because he did not reject my prayer
    or keep back his constant love from
        me.

A Song of Thanksgiving[k]

67 God, be merciful to us and bless
    us;
    look on us with kindness,
² so that the whole world may know your
        will;
    so that all nations may know your
        salvation.

³ May the peoples praise you, O God;
    may all the peoples praise you!

⁴ May the nations be glad and sing for
        joy,
    because you judge the peoples with
        justice
    and guide every nation on earth.

⁵ May the peoples praise you, O God;
    may all the peoples praise you!

⁶ The land has produced its harvest;
    God, our God, has blessed us.
⁷ God has blessed us;
    may all people everywhere honor
        him.

[k] HEBREW TITLE: *A psalm; a song.*

A National Song of Triumph[l]

68 God rises up and scatters his
        enemies.
    Those who hate him run away in
        defeat.
[2] As smoke is blown away, so he drives
        them off;
    as wax melts in front of the fire,
    so do the wicked perish in God's
        presence.
[3] But the righteous are glad and rejoice
        in his presence;
    they are happy and shout for joy.

[4] Sing to God, sing praises to his name;
    prepare a way for him who rides on
        the clouds.[m]
    His name is the LORD—be glad in his
        presence!

[5] God, who lives in his sacred Temple,
    cares for orphans and protects
        widows.
[6] He gives the lonely a home to live in
    and leads prisoners out into happy
        freedom,
    but rebels will have to live in a
        desolate land.

[7] O God, when you led your people,
    when you marched across the desert,
[8] the earth shook, and the sky poured
        down rain,
    because of the coming of the God of
        Sinai,[n]
    the coming of the God of Israel.
[9] You caused abundant rain to fall
    and restored your worn-out land;

[l] HEBREW TITLE: *A psalm by David; a song.*   [m] on the clouds; *or*
across the desert.   [n] GOD OF SINAI: *As the people of Israel went from
Egypt to Canaan, God revealed himself to them at Mount Sinai (see
Ex 19.16-25).*

¹⁰ your people made their home there;
in your goodness you provided for
the poor.

¹¹ The Lord gave the command,
and many women carried the news:
¹² "Kings and their armies are running
away!"
The women at home divided what
was captured:
¹³ figures of doves covered with silver,
whose wings glittered with fine gold.
(Why did some of you stay among the
sheep pens on the day of battle?)
¹⁴ When Almighty God scattered the
kings on Mount Zalmon,
he caused snow to fall there.

¹⁵ What a mighty mountain is Bashan,
a mountain of many peaks!
¹⁶ Why from your mighty peaks do you
look with scorn
on the mountainᵒ on which God
chose to live?
The LORD will live there forever!

¹⁷ With his many thousands of mighty
chariots
the Lord comes from Sinaiᵖ into the
holy place.
¹⁸ He goes up to the heights,
taking many captives with him;
he receives gifts from rebellious men.
The LORD God will live there.

¹⁹ Praise the Lord,
who carries our burdens day after
day;
he is the God who saves us.

ᵒ MOUNTAIN: See 2.6. ᵖ Probable text comes from Sinai; Hebrew in
them, Sinai.

20 Our God is a God who saves;
    he is the LORD, our Lord,
    who rescues us from death.

21 God will surely break the heads of his
        enemies,
    of those who persist in their sinful
        ways.
22 The Lord has said, "I will bring your
        enemies back from Bashan;
    I will bring them back from the
        depths of the ocean,
23 so that you may wade in their blood,
    and your dogs may lap up as much as
        they want."

24 O God, your march of triumph is seen
        by all,
    the procession of God, my king, into
        his sanctuary.
25 The singers are in front, the musicians
        are behind,
    in between are the girls beating the
        tambourines.
26 "Praise God in the meeting of his
        people;
    praise the LORD, all you descendants
        of Jacob!"
27 First comes Benjamin, the smallest
        tribe,
    then the leaders of Judah with their
        group,
    followed by the leaders of Zebulun
        and Naphtali.

28 Show your power, O God,
    the power you have used on our
        behalf
29 from your Temple in Jerusalem,
    where kings bring gifts to you.

³⁰ Rebuke Egypt, that wild animal in the
  reeds;
   rebuke the nations, that herd of bulls
    with their calves,
   until they all bow down and offer you
    their silver.
  Scatter those people who love to make
   war!^q
³¹ Ambassadors^r will come from Egypt;
   the Sudanese will raise their hands in
    prayer to God.

³² Sing to God, kingdoms of the world,
   sing praise to the Lord,
³³   to him who rides in the sky,
   the ancient sky.
  Listen to him shout with a mighty roar.
³⁴ Proclaim God's power;
   his majesty is over Israel,
   his might is in the skies.
³⁵ How awesome is God as he comes from
   his sanctuary—
   the God of Israel!
  He gives strength and power to his
   people.

  Praise God!

A Cry for Help^s

69 Save me, O God!
   The water is up to my neck;
² I am sinking in deep mud,
   and there is no solid ground;
  I am out in deep water,
   and the waves are about to drown
    me.
³ I am worn out from calling for help,
   and my throat is aching.
  I have strained my eyes,
   looking for your help.

^q Verse 30 in Hebrew is unclear. ^r Some ancient translations
Ambassadors; Hebrew unclear. ^s HEBREW TITLE: By David.

⁴ Those who hate me for no reason
  are more numerous than the hairs of
    my head.
My enemies tell lies against me;
  they are strong and want to kill me.
They made me give back things I did
    not steal.
⁵ My sins, O God, are not hidden from
    you;
  you know how foolish I have been.
⁶ Don't let me bring shame on those who
    trust in you,
    Sovereign LORD Almighty!
Don't let me bring disgrace to those
    who worship you,
    O God of Israel!
⁷ It is for your sake that I have been
    insulted
  and that I am covered with shame.
⁸ I am like a stranger to my brothers,
  like a foreigner to my family.

⁹ My devotion to your Temple burns in
    me like a fire;
  the insults which are hurled at you
    fall on me.
¹⁰ I humble myself' by fasting,
  and people insult me;
¹¹ I dress myself in clothes of mourning,
  and they laugh at me.
¹² They talk about me in the streets,
  and drunkards make up songs about
    me.

¹³ But as for me, I will pray to you, LORD;
  answer me, God, at a time you
    choose.
Answer me because of your great love,
  because you keep your promise to
    save.

' *Some ancient translations* humble myself; *Hebrew* cry.

14 Save me from sinking in the mud;
    keep me safe from my enemies,
    safe from the deep water.
15 Don't let the flood come over me;
    don't let me drown in the depths
    or sink into the grave.

16 Answer me, LORD, in the goodness of
    your constant love;
    in your great compassion turn to me!
17 Don't hide yourself from your servant;
    I am in great trouble—answer me
    now!
18 Come to me and save me;
    rescue me from my enemies.

19 You know how I am insulted,
    how I am disgraced and dishonored;
    you see all my enemies.
20 Insults have broken my heart,
    and I am in despair.
  I had hoped for sympathy, but there
    was none;
    for comfort, but I found none.
21 When I was hungry, they gave me
    poison;
    when I was thirsty, they offered me
    vinegar.

22 May their banquets cause their ruin;
    may their sacred feasts cause their
    downfall.
23 Strike them with blindness!
    Make their backs always weak!
24 Pour out your anger on them;
    let your indignation overtake them.
25 May their camps be left deserted;
    may no one be left alive in their
    tents.
26 They persecute those whom you have
    punished;
    they talk about the sufferings of those
    you have wounded.

27 Keep a record of all their sins;
   don't let them have any part in your
      salvation.
28 May their names be erased from the
      book of the living;
   may they not be included in the list
      of your people.

29 But I am in pain and despair;
   lift me up, O God, and save me!

30 I will praise God with a song;
   I will proclaim his greatness by
      giving him thanks.
31 This will please the LORD more than
      offering him cattle,
   more than sacrificing a full-grown
      bull.
32 When the oppressed see this, they will
      be glad;
   those who worship God will be
      encouraged.
33 The LORD listens to those in need
   and does not forget his people in
      prison.

34 Praise God, O heaven and earth,
   seas and all creatures in them.
35 He will save Jerusalem
   and rebuild the towns of Judah.
   His people will live there and possess
      the land;
36   the descendants of his servants will
      inherit it,
   and those who love him will live
      there.

A Prayer for Help "
(Psalm 40.13-17)

70 Save me, O God!
   LORD, help me now!

" HEBREW TITLE: *A psalm by David; a lament.*

² May those who try to kill me
    be defeated and confused.
May those who are happy because of
        my troubles
    be turned back and disgraced.
³ May those who make fun of me
    be dismayed by their defeat.

⁴ May all who come to you
    be glad and joyful.
May all who are thankful for your
        salvation
    always say, "How great is God!"

⁵ I am weak and poor;
    come to me quickly, O God.
You are my savior and my LORD—
    hurry to my aid!

An Old Man's Prayer

71 LORD, I have come to you for
        protection;
    never let me be defeated!
² Because you are righteous, help me and
        rescue me.
    Listen to me and save me!
³ Be my secure shelter
    and a strong fortressᵛ to protect me;
    you are my refuge and defense.

⁴ My God, rescue me from wicked men,
    from the power of cruel and evil men.
⁵ Sovereign LORD, I put my hope in you;
    I have trusted in you since I was
        young.
⁶ I have relied on you all my life;
    you have protectedʷ me since the day
        I was born.
    I will always praise you.

ᵛ *One ancient translation* a strong fortress; *Hebrew* to go always you commanded.   ʷ *Some ancient translations* protected; *Hebrew unclear.*

⁷ My life has been an example to many,
  because you have been my strong
  defender.
⁸ All day long I praise you
  and proclaim your glory.
⁹ Do not reject me now that I am old;
  do not abandon me now that I am
  feeble.
¹⁰ My enemies want to kill me;
  they talk and plot against me.
¹¹ They say, "God has abandoned him;
  let's go after him and catch him;
  there is no one to rescue him."

I am old and my hair is gray. (71.18)

12 Don't stay so far away, O God;
   my God, hurry to my aid!
13 May those who attack me
   be defeated and destroyed.
   May those who try to hurt me
   be shamed and disgraced.
14 I will always put my hope in you;
   I will praise you more and more.
15 I will tell of your goodness;
   all day long I will speak of your
       salvation,
   though it is more than I can
       understand.
16 I will praise your power, Sovereign
       LORD;
   I will proclaim your goodness, yours
       alone.

17 You have taught me ever since I was
       young,
   and I still tell of your wonderful acts.
18 Now that I am old and my hair is gray,
   do not abandon me, O God!
   Be with me while I proclaim your
       power and might
   to all generations to come.

19 Your righteousness, God, reaches the
       skies.
   You have done great things;
   there is no one like you.
20 You have sent troubles and suffering on
       me,
   but you will restore my strength;
   you will keep me from the grave.
21 You will make me greater than ever;
   you will comfort me again.

22 I will indeed praise you with the harp;
   I will praise your faithfulness, my
       God.
   On my harp I will play hymns to you,
   the Holy One of Israel.

²³ I will shout for joy as I play for you;
 with my whole being I will sing
 because you have saved me.
²⁴ I will speak of your righteousness all
 day long,
 because those who tried to harm me
 have been defeated and disgraced.

A Prayer for the King^x

72 Teach the king to judge with your
 righteousness, O God;
 share with him your own justice,
² so that he will rule over your people
 with justice
 and govern the oppressed with
 righteousness.
³ May the land enjoy prosperity;
 may it experience righteousness.
⁴ May the king judge the poor fairly;
 may he help the needy
 and defeat their oppressors.
⁵ May your people worship you as long
 as the sun shines,
 as long as the moon gives light, for
 ages to come.

⁶ May the king be like rain on the fields,
 like showers falling on the land.
⁷ May righteousness flourish in his
 lifetime,
 and may prosperity last as long as the
 moon gives light.

⁸ His kingdom will reach from sea to sea,
 from the Euphrates to the ends of the
 earth.
⁹ The peoples of the desert will bow
 down before him;
 his enemies will throw themselves to
 the ground.

^x HEBREW TITLE: *By Solomon.*

¹⁰ The kings of Spain and of the islands
       will offer him gifts;
    the kings of Arabia and Ethiopia will
       bring him offerings.
¹¹ All kings will bow down before him;
    all nations will serve him.

¹² He rescues the poor who call to him,
    and those who are needy and
      neglected.
¹³ He has pity on the weak and poor;
    he saves the lives of those in need.
¹⁴ He rescues them from oppression and
      violence;
    their lives are precious to him.

¹⁵ Long live the king!
    May he be given gold from Arabia;
    may prayers be said for him at all
      times;
    may God's blessings be on him
      always!
¹⁶ May there be plenty of grain in the
      land;
    may the hills be covered with crops,
    as fruitful as those of Lebanon.
May the cities be filled with people,
    like fields full of grass.
¹⁷ May the king's name never be
      forgotten;
    may his fame last as long as the sun.
May all nations ask God to bless them
as he has blessed the king.^s

¹⁸ Praise the LORD, the God of Israel!
He alone does these wonderful things.
¹⁹ Praise his glorious name forever!
May his glory fill the whole world.

Amen! Amen!

^s as he has blessed the king; *or* and may they wish happiness for
the king.

²⁰ This is the end of the prayers of David
son of Jesse.

BOOK THREE
(Psalms 73—89)

The Justice of God^y

73 God is indeed good to Israel,
to those who have pure hearts.
² But I had nearly lost confidence;
my faith was almost gone
³ because I was jealous of the proud
when I saw that things go well for the
wicked.

⁴ They do not suffer pain;
they are strong and healthy.
⁵ They do not suffer as other people do;
they do not have the troubles that
others have.
⁶ And so they wear pride like a necklace
and violence like a robe;
⁷ their hearts pour out evil,^z
and their minds are busy with wicked
schemes.
⁸ They laugh at other people and speak
of evil things;
they are proud and make plans to
oppress others.
⁹ They speak evil of God in heaven
and give arrogant orders to men on
earth,
¹⁰ so that even God's people turn to them
and eagerly believe whatever they
say.^a
¹¹ They say, "God will not know;
the Most High will not find out."
¹² That is what the wicked are like.
They have plenty and are always
getting more.

^y HEBREW TITLE: *By Asaph.*   ^z *Some ancient translations* their hearts
pour out evil; *Hebrew unclear.*   ^a *Verse 10 in Hebrew is unclear.*

¹³ Is it for nothing, then, that I have kept
     myself pure
     and have not committed sin?
¹⁴ O God, you have made me suffer all
     day long;
     every morning you have punished
     me.

¹⁵ If I had said such things,
     I would not be acting as one of your
     people.
¹⁶ I tried to think this problem through,
     but it was too difficult for me
¹⁷   until I went into your Temple.
Then I understood what will happen to
     the wicked.

¹⁸ You will put them in slippery places
     and make them fall to destruction!
¹⁹ They are instantly destroyed;
     they go down to a horrible end.
²⁰ They are like a dream that goes away in
     the morning;
     when you rouse yourself, O Lord,
     they disappear.

²¹ When my thoughts were bitter
     and my feelings were hurt,
²² I was as stupid as an animal;
     I did not understand you.
²³ Yet I always stay close to you,
     and you hold me by the hand.
²⁴ You guide me with your instruction
     and at the end you will receive me
     with honor.
²⁵ What else do I have in heaven but you?
     Since I have you, what else could I
     want on earth?
²⁶ My mind and my body may grow weak,
     but God is my strength;
     he is all I ever need.

²⁷ Those who abandon you will certainly
        perish;
    you will destroy those who are
        unfaithful to you.
²⁸ But as for me, how wonderful to be
        near God,
    to find protection with the Lord GOD
    and to proclaim all that he has done!

A Prayer for National Deliverance[b]

74 Why have you abandoned us like
        this, O God?
    Will you be angry with your own
        people forever?
² Remember your people, whom you
        chose for yourself long ago,
    whom you brought out of slavery to
        be your own tribe.
    Remember Mount Zion, where once
        you lived.
³ Walk over these total ruins;
    our enemies have destroyed
        everything in the Temple.

⁴ Your enemies have shouted in triumph
        in your Temple;
    they have placed their flags there as
        signs of victory.
⁵ They looked like woodsmen
    cutting down trees with their axes.[c]
⁶ They smashed all the wooden panels
    with their axes and sledge hammers.
⁷ They wrecked your Temple and set it
        on fire;
    they desecrated the place where you
        are worshiped.
⁸ They wanted to crush us completely;
    they burned down every holy place in
        the land.

[b] HEBREW TITLE: *A poem by Asaph.*   [c] *Verse 5 in Hebrew is unclear.*

⁹ All our sacred symbols are gone;
    there are no prophets left,
    and no one knows how long this will
      last.
¹⁰ How long, O God, will our enemies
      laugh at you?
    Will they insult your name forever?
¹¹ Why have you refused to help us?
    Why do you keep your hands behind
      you?ᵈ

¹² But you have been our king from the
      beginning, O God;
    you have saved us many times.
¹³ With your mighty strength you divided
      the sea
    and smashed the heads of the sea
      monsters;
¹⁴ you crushed the heads of the monster
      Leviathanᵉ
    and fed his body to desert animals.ᶠ
¹⁵ You made springs and fountains flow;
    you dried up large rivers.
¹⁶ You created the day and the night;
    you set the sun and the moon in their
      places;
¹⁷ you set the limits of the earth;
    you made summer and winter.

¹⁸ But remember, O Lᴏʀᴅ, that your
      enemies laugh at you,
    that they are godless and despise you.
¹⁹ Don't abandon your helpless people to
      their cruel enemies;
    don't forget your persecuted people!

²⁰ Remember the covenant you made with
      us.
    There is violence in every dark
      corner of the land.

ᵈ *Probable text* Why do you keep your hands behind you; *Hebrew unclear.* ᵉ ʟᴇᴠɪᴀᴛʜᴀɴ: *A legendary monster which was a symbol of the forces of chaos and evil.* ᶠ animals; *or* people.

21 Don't let the oppressed be put to
    shame;
  let those poor and needy people
    praise you.

22 Rouse yourself, God, and defend your
    cause!
  Remember that godless people laugh
    at you all day long.
23 Don't forget the angry shouts of your
    enemies,
  the continuous noise made by your
    foes.

God the Judge[g]

75   We give thanks to you, O God,
     we give thanks to you!
We proclaim how great you are
and tell of[h] the wonderful things you
    have done.

2 "I have set a time for judgment," says
    God,
  "and I will judge with fairness.
3 Though every living creature tremble
  and the earth itself be shaken,
  I will keep its foundations firm.
4 I tell the wicked not to be arrogant;
5   I tell them to stop their boasting."

6 Judgment does not come from the east
    or from the west,
  from the north or from the south;[i]
7 it is God who is the judge,
  condemning some and acquitting
    others.

---

[g] HEBREW TITLE: *A psalm by Asaph; a song.*   [h] *Some ancient
translations* We proclaim how great you are and tell of; *Hebrew*
Your name is near and they tell of.   [i] *Probable text* from the north
or from the south; *Hebrew* from the wilderness of the mountains.

8 The LORD holds a cup in his hand,
    filled with the strong wine of his
        anger.
He pours it out, and all the wicked
    drink it;
    they drink it down to the last drop.

9 But I will never stop speaking of the
    God of Jacob
    or singing praises to him.
10 He will break the power of the wicked,
    but the power of the righteous will be
        increased.

God the Victor [j]

76 God is known in Judah;
        his name is honored in Israel.
2 He has his home in Jerusalem;
    he lives on Mount Zion.
3 There he broke the arrows of the
        enemy,
    their shields and swords, yes, all their
        weapons.

4 How glorious you are, O God!
    How majestic, as you return from the
        mountains
    where you defeated your foes.
5 Their brave soldiers have been stripped
        of all they had
    and now are sleeping the sleep of
        death;
    all their strength and skill was
        useless.
6 When you threatened them, O God of
        Jacob,
    the horses and their riders fell dead.

7 But you, LORD, are feared by all.
    No one can stand in your presence
    when you are angry.

----

[j] HEBREW TITLE: *A psalm by Asaph; a song.*

⁸ You made your judgment known from
     heaven;
   the world was afraid and kept silent,
⁹ when you rose up to pronounce
     judgment,
   to save all the oppressed on earth.

¹⁰ Men's anger only results in more praise
     for you;
   those who survive the wars will keep
     your festivals.ᵏ

¹¹ Give the LORD your God what you
     promised him;
   bring gifts to him, all you nearby
     nations.
   God makes men fear him;
¹²   he humbles proud princes
     and terrifies great kings.

Comfort in Time of Distressˡ

77 I cry aloud to God;
       I cry aloud, and he hears me.
² In times of trouble I pray to the Lord;
   all night long I lift my hands in
     prayer,
   but I cannot find comfort.
³ When I think of God, I sigh;
   when I meditate, I feel discouraged.

⁴ He keeps me awake all night;
   I am so worried that I cannot speak.
⁵ I think of days gone by
   and remember years of long ago.
⁶ I spend the night in deep thought;ᵐ
   I meditate, and this is what I ask
     myself:

ᵏ *One ancient translation* will keep your festivals; *verse 10 in Hebrew
is unclear.* ˡ HEBREW TITLE: *A psalm by Asaph.* ᵐ *Some ancient
translations* deep thought; *Hebrew* song.

7 "Will the Lord always reject us?
    Will he never again be pleased with
        us?
8 Has he stopped loving us?
    Does his promise no longer stand?
9 Has God forgotten to be merciful?
    Has anger taken the place of his
        compassion?"
' Then I said, "What hurts me most is
        this—
    that God is no longer powerful."ⁿ

I will remember your great deeds,
    LORD;
    I will recall the wonders you did in
        the past.
I will think about all that you have
        done;
    I will meditate on all your mighty
        acts.

Everything you do, O God, is holy.
    No god is as great as you.
You are the God who works miracles;
    you showed your might among the
        nations.
15 By your power you saved your people,
    the descendants of Jacob and of
        Joseph.

16 When the waters saw you, O God, they
        were afraid,
    and the depths of the sea trembled.
17 The clouds poured down rain;
    thunder crashed from the sky,
    and lightning flashed in all directions.
18 The crash of your thunder rolled out,
    and flashes of lightning lit up the
        world;
    the earth trembled and shook.

ⁿ Verse 10 in Hebrew is unclear.

¹⁹ You walked through the waves;
     you crossed the deep sea,
     but your footprints could not be seen.
²⁰ You led your people like a shepherd,
     with Moses and Aaron in charge.

God and His People[o]

78 Listen, my people, to my
           teaching,
     and pay attention to what I say.
² I am going to use wise sayings
     and explain mysteries from the past,
³   things we have heard and known,
     things that our fathers told us.
⁴ We will not keep them from our
       children;
     we will tell the next generation
     about the LORD's power and his great
       deeds
     and the wonderful things he has
       done.

⁵ He gave laws to the people of Israel
     and commandments to the
       descendants of Jacob.
 He instructed our ancestors
     to teach his laws to their children,
⁶ so that the next generation might learn
       them
     and in turn should tell their children.
⁷ In this way they also will put their trust
       in God
     and not forget what he has done,
     but always obey his commandments.
⁸ They will not be like their ancestors,
     a rebellious and disobedient people,
 whose trust in God was never firm
     and who did not remain faithful to
       him.

[o] HEBREW TITLE: *A poem by Asaph.*

9 The Ephraimites, armed with bows and
  arrows,
    ran away on the day of battle.
10 They did not keep their covenant with
   God;
     they refused to obey his law.
11 They forgot what he had done,
     the miracles they had seen him
     perform.
12 While their ancestors watched, God
   performed miracles
     in the plain of Zoan in the land of
     Egypt.
13 He divided the sea and took them
   through it;
     he made the waters stand like walls.
14 By day he led them with a cloud
     and all night long with the light of a
     fire.
15 He split rocks open in the desert
     and gave them water from the depths.
16 He caused a stream to come out of the
   rock
     and made water flow like a river.

17 But they continued to sin against God,
     and in the desert they rebelled against
     the Most High.
18 They deliberately put God to the test
     by demanding the food they wanted.
19 They spoke against God and said,
     "Can God supply food in the desert?
20 It is true that he struck the rock,
     and water flowed out in a torrent;
   but can he also provide us with bread
     and give his people meat?"

21 And so the LORD was angry when he
   heard them;
     he attacked his people with fire,
     and his anger against them grew,

22 because they had no faith in him
    and did not believe that he would
        save them.
23 But he spoke to the sky above
    and commanded its doors to open;
24 he gave them grain from heaven,
    by sending down manna for them to
        eat.
25 So they ate the food of angels,
    and God gave them all they wanted.
26 He also caused the east wind to blow,
    and by his power he stirred up the
        south wind;
27 and to his people he sent down birds,
    as many as the grains of sand on the
        shore;
28 they fell in the middle of the camp
    all around the tents.
29 So the people ate and were satisfied;
    God gave them what they wanted.
30 But they had not yet satisfied their
        craving
    and were still eating,
31 when God became angry with them
    and killed their strongest men,
    the best young men of Israel.

32 In spite of all this the people kept
        sinning;
    in spite of his miracles they did not
        trust him.
33 So he ended their days like a breath
    and their lives with sudden disaster.
34 Whenever he killed some of them,
    the rest would turn to him;
    they would repent and pray earnestly
        to him.
35 They remembered that God was their
        protector,
    that the Almighty came to their aid.
36 But their words were all lies;
    nothing they said was sincere.

³⁷ They were not loyal to him;
    they were not faithful to their
       covenant with him.

³⁸ But God was merciful to his people.
    He forgave their sin
    and did not destroy them.
Many times he held back his anger
    and restrained his fury.
³⁹ He remembered that they were only
       mortal beings,
    like a wind that blows by and is gone.

⁴⁰ How often they rebelled against him in
       the desert;
    how many times they made him sad!
⁴¹ Again and again they put God to the
       test
    and brought pain to the Holy God of
       Israel.
⁴² They forgot his great power
    and the day when he saved them
       from their enemies
⁴³   and performed his mighty acts and
       miracles
    in the plain of Zoan in the land of
       Egypt.
⁴⁴ He turned the rivers into blood,
    and the Egyptians had no water to
       drink.
⁴⁵ He sent flies among them, that
       tormented them,
    and frogs that ruined their land.
⁴⁶ He sent locusts to eat their crops
    and to destroy their fields.
⁴⁷ He killed their grapevines with hail
    and their fig trees with frost.
⁴⁸ He killed their cattle with hail
    and their flocks with lightning.ᵖ

ᵖ hail . . . lightning; or terrible disease . . . deadly plague.

⁴⁹ He caused them great distress
by pouring out his anger and fierce
rage,
which came as messengers of death.
⁵⁰ He did not restrain his anger
or spare their lives,
but killed them with a plague.
⁵¹ He killed the first-born sons
of all the families of Egypt.

⁵² Then he led his people out like a
shepherd
and guided them through the desert.
⁵³ He led them safely, and they were not
afraid;
but the sea came rolling over their
enemies.
⁵⁴ He brought them to his holy land,
to the mountains which he himself
conquered.
⁵⁵ He drove out the inhabitants as his
people advanced;
he divided their land among the
tribes of Israel
and gave their homes to his people.

⁵⁶ But they rebelled against Almighty God
and put him to the test.
They did not obey his commandments,
⁵⁷   but were rebellious and disloyal like
their fathers,
unreliable as a crooked arrow.
⁵⁸ They angered him with their heathen
places of worship,
and with their idols they made him
furious.
⁵⁹ God was angry when he saw it,
so he rejected his people completely.
⁶⁰ He abandoned his tent in Shiloh,ᵃ
the home where he had lived among
us.

ᵃ SHILOH: *The central place of worship for the people of Israel before
the time of King David.*

⁶¹ He allowed our enemies to capture the
      Covenant Box,
    the symbol of his power and glory.
⁶² He was angry with his own people
    and let them be killed by their
      enemies.
⁶³ Young men were killed in war,
    and young women had no one to
      marry.
⁶⁴ Priests died by violence,
    and their widows were not allowed to
      mourn.

⁶⁵ At last the Lord woke up as though
      from sleep;
    he was like a strong man excited by
      wine.
⁶⁶ He drove his enemies back
    in lasting and shameful defeat.
⁶⁷ But he rejected the descendants of
      Joseph;
    he did not select the tribe of
      Ephraim.
⁶⁸ Instead he chose the tribe of Judah
    and Mount Zion, which he dearly
      loves.
⁶⁹ There he built his Temple
    like his home in heaven;
  he made it firm like the earth itself,
    secure for all time.

⁷⁰ He chose his servant David;
    he took him from the pastures,
⁷¹   where he looked after his flocks,
    and he made him king of Israel,
    the shepherd of the people of God.
⁷² David took care of them with unselfish
      devotion
    and led them with skill.

A Prayer for the Nation's Deliverance'

79 O God, the heathen have invaded
    your land.
    They have desecrated your holy
        Temple
    and left Jerusalem in ruins.
2 They left the bodies of your people for
    the vultures,
        the bodies of your servants for wild
        animals to eat.
3 They shed your people's blood like
    water;
        blood flowed like water all through
        Jerusalem,
        and no one was left to bury the dead.
4 The surrounding nations insult us;
        they laugh at us and mock us.

5 LORD, will you be angry with us
    forever?
        Will your anger continue to burn like
        fire?
6 Turn your anger on the nations that do
    not worship you,
        on the people who do not pray to
        you.
7 For they have killed your people;
        they have ruined your country.

8 Do not punish us for the sins of our
    ancestors.
        Have mercy on us now;
        we have lost all hope.
9 Help us, O God, and save us;
        rescue us and forgive our sins
        for the sake of your own honor.
10 Why should the nations ask us,
    "Where is your God?"
    Let us see you punish the nations
        for shedding the blood of your
        servants.

' HEBREW TITLE: *A psalm by Asaph.*

¹¹ Listen to the groans of the prisoners,
and by your great power free those
who are condemned to die.
¹² Lord, pay the other nations back seven
times
for all the insults they have hurled at
you.
¹³ Then we, your people, the sheep of
your flock,
will thank you forever
and praise you for all time to come.

A Prayer for the Nation's Restoration ⁵

80 Listen to us, O Shepherd of
Israel;
hear us, leader of your flock.
Seated on your throne above the
winged creatures,
²   reveal yourself to the tribes of
Ephraim, Benjamin, and Manasseh.
Show us your strength;
come and save us!

³ Bring us back, O God!
Show us your mercy, and we will be
saved!

⁴ How much longer, LORD God
Almighty,
will you be angry with your people's
prayers?
⁵ You have given us sorrow to eat,
a large cup of tears to drink.
⁶ You let the surrounding nations fight
over our land;
our enemies insult us.

⁷ Bring us back, Almighty God!
Show us your mercy, and we will be
saved!

⁵ HEBREW TITLE: *A psalm by Asaph; a testimony.*

8 You brought a grapevine out of Egypt;
   you drove out other nations and
      planted it in their land.
9 You cleared a place for it to grow;
   its roots went deep, and it spread out
      over the whole land.
10 It covered the hills with its shade;
   its branches overshadowed the giant
      cedars.
11 It extended its branches to the
      Mediterranean Sea
   and as far as the Euphrates River.
12 Why did you break down the fences
      around it?
   Now anyone passing by can steal its
      grapes;
13   wild hogs trample it down,
   and wild animals feed on it.

14 Turn to us, Almighty God!
   Look down from heaven at us;
   come and save your people!
15 Come and save this grapevine that you
      planted,
   this young vine you made grow so
      strong!

16 Our enemies have set it on fire and cut
      it down;
   look at them in anger and destroy
      them!
17 Preserve and protect the people you
      have chosen,
   the nation you made so strong.
18 We will never turn away from you
      again;
   keep us alive, and we will praise you.

19 Bring us back, LORD God Almighty.
   Show us your mercy, and we will be
      saved.

A Song for a Festival[^1]

81   Shout for joy to God our
          defender;
      sing praise to the God of Jacob!
2 Start the music and beat the
          tambourines;
      play pleasant music on the harps and
          the lyres.
3 Blow the trumpet for the festival,
      when the moon is new and when the
          moon is full.
4 This is the law in Israel,
      an order from the God of Jacob.
5 He gave it to the people of Israel
      when he attacked the land of Egypt.

  I hear an unknown voice saying,
6 "I took the burdens off your backs;
      I let you put down your loads of
          bricks.
7 When you were in trouble, you called
          to me, and I saved you.
      From my hiding place in the storm, I
          answered you.
      I put you to the test at the springs of
          Meribah.
8 Listen, my people, to my warning;
      Israel, how I wish you would listen to
          me!
9 You must never worship another god.
10 I am the LORD your God,
      who brought you out of Egypt.
  Open your mouth, and I will feed you.

11 "But my people would not listen to me;
      Israel would not obey me.
12 So I let them go their stubborn ways
      and do whatever they wanted.

[^1]: HEBREW TITLE: *By Asaph.*

13 How I wish my people would listen to
      me;
    how I wish they would obey me!
14 I would quickly defeat their enemies
      and conquer all their foes.
15 Those who hate me would bow in fear
      before me;
    their punishment would last forever.
16 But I would feed you with the finest
      wheat
    and satisfy you with wild honey."

God the Supreme Ruler[u]

82 God presides in the heavenly
      council;
    in the assembly of the gods he gives
      his decision:
2 "You must stop judging unjustly;
    you must no longer be partial to the
      wicked!
3 Defend the rights of the poor and the
      orphans;
    be fair to the needy and the helpless.
4 Rescue them from the power of evil
      men.

5 "How ignorant you are! How stupid!
    You are completely corrupt,
    and justice has disappeared from the
      world.
6 'You are gods,' I said;
    'all of you are sons of the Most High.'
7 But you will die like men;
    your life will end like that of any
      prince."

8 Come, O God, and rule the world;
    all the nations are yours.

---

[u] HEBREW TITLE: *A psalm by Asaph.*

A Prayer for the Defeat of Israel's Enemies[v]

83 O God, do not keep silent;
      do not be still, do not be quiet!
2 Look! Your enemies are in revolt,
      and those who hate you are rebelling.
3 They are making secret plans against
         your people;
      they are plotting against those you
         protect.
4 "Come," they say, "let us destroy their
         nation,
      so that Israel will be forgotten
         forever."

5 They agree on their plan
      and form an alliance against you:
6 the people of Edom and the
         Ishmaelites;
      the people of Moab and the Hagrites;
7 the people of Gebal, Ammon, and
         Amalek,
      and of Philistia and Tyre.
8 Assyria has also joined them
      as a strong ally of the Ammonites
         and Moabites, the descendants of
         Lot.

9 Do to them what you did to the
         Midianites,
      and to Sisera and Jabin at the Kishon
         River.
10 You defeated them at Endor,
      and their bodies rotted on the ground.
11 Do to their leaders what you did to
         Oreb and Zeeb;
      defeat all their rulers as you did
         Zebah and Zalmunna,
12 who said, "We will take for our own
      the land that belongs to God."

13 Scatter them like dust, O God,
      like straw blown away by the wind.

---

[v] HEBREW TITLE: *A psalm by Asaph; a song.*

14 As fire burns the forest,
    as flames set the hills on fire,
15 chase them away with your storm
    and terrify them with your fierce
        winds.
16 Cover their faces with shame, O LORD,
    and make them acknowledge your
        power.
17 May they be defeated and terrified
        forever;
    may they die in complete disgrace.
18 May they know that you alone are the
        LORD,
    supreme ruler over all the earth.

Longing for God's House[w]

84 How I love your Temple, LORD
        Almighty!
2   How I want to be there!
    I long to be in the LORD's Temple.
    With my whole being I sing for joy
        to the living God.
3 Even the sparrows have built a nest,
    and the swallows have their own
        home;
    they keep their young near your altars,
        LORD Almighty, my king and my
            God.
4 How happy are those who live in your
        Temple,
    always singing praise to you.

5 How happy are those whose strength
        comes from you,
    who are eager to make the pilgrimage
        to Mount Zion.
6 As they pass through the dry valley of
        Baca,
    it becomes a place of springs;
    the early rain fills it with pools.

[w] HEBREW TITLE: *A psalm by the clan of Korah.*

⁷ They grow stronger as they go;
      they will see the God of gods on
          Zion.

⁸ Hear my prayer, Lord God Almighty.
      Listen, O God of Jacob!
⁹ Bless our king, O God,
      the king you have chosen.

¹⁰ One day spent in your Temple
      is better than a thousand anywhere
          else;
   I would rather stand at the gate of the
      house of my God
      than live in the homes of the wicked.
¹¹ The Lord is our protector and glorious
      king,
      blessing us with kindness and honor.
   He does not refuse any good thing
      to those who do what is right.
¹² Lord Almighty, how happy are those
      who trust in you!

A Prayer for the Nation's Welfare ˣ

85 Lord, you have been merciful to
      your land;
   you have made Israel prosperous
      again.
² You have forgiven your people's sins
      and pardoned all their wrongs.
³ You stopped being angry with them
      and held back your furious rage.

⁴ Bring us back, O God our savior,
      and stop being displeased with us!
⁵ Will you be angry with us forever?
      Will your anger never cease?
⁶ Make us strong again,
      and we, your people, will praise you.

ˣ HEBREW TITLE: *A psalm by the clan of Korah.*

⁷ Show us your constant love, O LORD,
    and give us your saving help.

⁸ I am listening to what the LORD God is
        saying;
    he promises peace to us, his own
        people,
    if we do not go back to our foolish
        ways.
⁹ Surely he is ready to save those who
        honor him,
    and his saving presence will remain
        in our land.

¹⁰ Love and faithfulness will meet;
    righteousness and peace will embrace.
¹¹ Man's loyalty will reach up from the
        earth,
    and God's righteousness will look
        down from heaven.
¹² The LORD will make us prosperous,
    and our land will produce rich
        harvests.
¹³ Righteousness will go before the LORD
    and prepare the path for him.

A Prayer for Help ʸ

86 Listen to me, LORD, and answer
        me,
    for I am helpless and weak.
² Save me from death, because I am loyal
        to you;
    save me, for I am your servant and I
        trust in you.

³ You are my God, so be merciful to me;
    I pray to you all day long.
⁴ Make your servant glad, O Lord,
    because my prayers go up to you.

ʸ HEBREW TITLE: *A prayer by David.*

⁵ You are good to us and forgiving,
    full of constant love for all who pray
        to you.

⁶ Listen, LORD, to my prayer;
    hear my cries for help.
⁷ I call to you in times of trouble,
    because you answer my prayers.

⁸ There is no god like you, O Lord,
    not one has done what you have
        done.
⁹ All the nations that you have created
    will come and bow down to you;
    they will praise your greatness.
¹⁰ You are mighty and do wonderful
        things;
    you alone are God.

¹¹ Teach me, LORD, what you want me to
        do,
    and I will obey you faithfully;
    teach me to serve you with complete
        devotion.
¹² I will praise you with all my heart, O
        Lord my God;
    I will proclaim your greatness
        forever.
¹³ How great is your constant love for me!
    You have saved me from the grave
        itself.
¹⁴ Proud men are coming against me, O
        God;
    a gang of cruel men is trying to kill
        me—
    people who pay no attention to you.
¹⁵ But you, O Lord, are a merciful and
        loving God,
    always patient, always kind and
        faithful.

¹⁶ Turn to me and have mercy on me;
  strengthen me and save me,
  because I serve you just as my
    mother did.
¹⁷ Show me proof of your goodness,
    LORD;
  those who hate me will be ashamed
  when they see that you have given
    me comfort and help.

In Praise of Jerusalem ᶻ

87 The LORD built his city on the
         sacred hill;ᵃ
² more than any other place in Israel
  he loves the city of Jerusalem.
³ Listen, city of God,
  to the wonderful things he says about
    you:

⁴ "I will include Egypt and Babylonia
  when I list the nations that obey me;
  the people of Philistia, Tyre, and Sudan
  I will number among the inhabitants
    of Jerusalem."

⁵ Of Zion it will be said
  that all nations belong there
  and that the Almighty will make her
    strong.
⁶ The LORD will write a list of the
    peoples
  and include them all as citizens of
    Jerusalem.
⁷ They dance and sing,
  "In Zion is the source of all our
    blessings."

ᶻ HEBREW TITLE: *A psalm by the clan of Korah; a song.*   ᵃ SACRED
HILL: *See 2.6.*

A Cry for Help*b*

88 LORD God, my savior, I cry out
all day,
and at night I come before you.
2 Hear my prayer;
listen to my cry for help!

3 So many troubles have fallen on me
that I am close to death.
4 I am like all others who are about to
die;
all my strength is gone.*c*
5 I am abandoned among the dead;
I am like the slain lying in their
graves,
those you have forgotten completely,
who are beyond your help.
6 You have thrown me into the depths of
the tomb,
into the darkest and deepest pit.
7 Your anger lies heavy on me,
and I am crushed beneath its waves.

8 You have caused my friends to abandon
me;
you have made me repulsive to them.
I am closed in and cannot escape;
9   my eyes are weak from suffering.
LORD, every day I call to you
and lift my hands to you in prayer.

10 Do you perform miracles for the dead?
Do they rise up and praise you?
11 Is your constant love spoken of in the
grave
or your faithfulness in the place of
destruction?

---

b HEBREW TITLE: *A psalm by the clan of Korah; a song. A poem by
Heman the Ezrahite.* *c* all my strength is gone; *or* there is no help
for me.

¹² Are your miracles seen in that place of
     darkness
     or your goodness in the land of the
        forgotten?

¹³ LORD, I call to you for help;
     every morning I pray to you.
¹⁴ Why do you reject me, LORD?
     Why do you turn away from me?
¹⁵ Ever since I was young, I have suffered
     and been near death;
     I am worn out*d* from the burden of
        your punishments.
¹⁶ Your furious anger crushes me;
     your terrible attacks destroy me.
¹⁷ All day long they surround me like a
     flood;
     they close in on me from every side.
¹⁸ You have made even my closest friends
     abandon me,
     and darkness is my only companion.

A Hymn in Time of National Trouble*e*

89 O LORD, I will always sing of
        your constant love;
     I will proclaim your faithfulness
        forever.
² I know that your love will last for all
     time,
     that your faithfulness is as permanent
        as the sky.
³ You said, "I have made a covenant
     with the man I chose;
     I have promised my servant David,
⁴ 'A descendant of yours will always be
     king;
     I will preserve your dynasty
        forever.' "

d Probable text I am worn out; *Hebrew unclear.* *e* HEBREW TITLE: *A
poem by Ethan the Ezrahite.*

⁵ The heavens sing of the wonderful
        things you do;
    the holy ones sing of your
        faithfulness, LORD.
⁶ No one in heaven is like you, LORD;
    none of the heavenly beings is your
        equal.
⁷ You are feared in the council of the
        holy ones;
    they all stand in awe of you.

⁸ LORD God Almighty, none is as mighty
        as you;
    in all things you are faithful, O LORD.
⁹ You rule over the powerful sea;
    you calm its angry waves.
¹⁰ You crushed the monster Rahab*f* and
        killed it;
    with your mighty strength you
        defeated your enemies.
¹¹ Heaven is yours, the earth also;
    you made the world and everything
        in it.
¹² You created the north and the south;
    Mount Tabor and Mount Hermon
        sing to you for joy.
¹³ How powerful you are!
    How great is your strength!
¹⁴ Your kingdom is founded on
        righteousness and justice;
    love and faithfulness are shown in all
        you do.

¹⁵ How happy are the people who
        worship you with songs,
    who live in the light of your kindness!
¹⁶ Because of you they rejoice all day
        long,
    and they praise you for your
        goodness.
¹⁷ You give us great victories;
    in your love you make us triumphant.

f RAHAB: *A legendary sea monster which represented the forces of
chaos and evil.*

¹⁸ You, O LORD, chose our protector;
   you, the Holy God of Israel, gave us
      our king.

God's Promise to David

¹⁹ In a vision long ago you said to your
      faithful servants,
   "I have given help to a famous
      soldier;
   I have given the throne to one I
      chose from the people.
²⁰ I have made my servant David king
   by anointing him with holy oil.
²¹ My strength will always be with him,
   my power will make him strong.
²² His enemies will never succeed against
      him;
   the wicked will not defeat him.
²³ I will crush his foes
   and kill everyone who hates him.
²⁴ I will love him and be loyal to him;
   I will make him always victorious.
²⁵ I will extend his kingdom
   from the Mediterranean to the
      Euphrates River.
²⁶ He will say to me,
   'You are my father and my God;
   you are my protector and savior.'
²⁷ I will make him my first-born son,
   the greatest of all kings.
²⁸ I will always keep my promise to him,
   and my covenant with him will last
      forever.
²⁹ His dynasty will be as permanent as the
      sky;
   a descendant of his will always be
      king.

³⁰ "But if his descendants disobey my law
   and do not live according to my
      commands,

³¹ if they disregard my instructions
  and do not keep my commandments,
³² then I will punish them for their sins;
  I will make them suffer for their
    wrongs.
³³ But I will not stop loving David
  or fail to keep my promise to him.
³⁴ I will not break my covenant with him
  or take back even one promise I
    made him.

³⁵ "Once and for all I have promised by
    my holy name:
  I will never lie to David.
³⁶ He will always have descendants,
  and I will watch over his kingdom as
    long as the sun shines.
³⁷ It will be as permanent as the moon,
  that faithful witness in the sky."

Lament over the Defeat of the King

³⁸ But you are angry with your chosen
    king;
  you have deserted and rejected him.
³⁹ You have broken your covenant with
    your servant
  and thrown his crown in the dirt.
⁴⁰ You have torn down the walls of his
    city
  and left his forts in ruins.
⁴¹ All who pass by steal his belongings;
  all his neighbors laugh at him.
⁴² You have given the victory to his
    enemies;
  you have made them all happy.
⁴³ You have made his weapons useless
  and let him be defeated in battle.
⁴⁴ You have taken away his royal scepter[g]
  and knocked his throne to the
    ground.

_____

[g] *Probable text* royal scepter; *Hebrew* purity.

⁴⁵ You have made him old before his time
    and covered him with disgrace.

A Prayer for Deliverance

⁴⁶ LORD, will you hide yourself forever?
    How long will your anger burn like
        fire?
⁴⁷ Remember how short my life is;
    remember that you created all of us
        mortal!
⁴⁸ Who can live and never die?
    How can man keep himself from the
        grave?

⁴⁹ Lord, where are the former proofs of
        your love?
    Where are the promises you made to
        David?
⁵⁰ Don't forget how I, your servant, am
        insulted,
    how I endure all the curses ʰ of the
        heathen.
⁵¹ Your enemies insult your chosen king,
        O LORD!
    They insult him wherever he goes.

⁵² Praise the LORD forever!

        Amen! Amen!

BOOK FOUR
(Psalms 90—106)

Of God and Man ⁱ

90 O Lord, you have always been
        our home.
² Before you created the hills
    or brought the world into being,
    you were eternally God,
    and will be God forever.

ʰ *Probable text* curses; *Hebrew* crowds.   ⁱ HEBREW TITLE: *A prayer by Moses, the man of God.*

³ You tell man to return to what he was;
    you change him back to dust.
⁴ A thousand years to you are like one
       day;
    they are like yesterday, already gone,
    like a short hour in the night.
⁵ You carry us away like a flood;
    we last no longer than a dream.
  We are like weeds that sprout in the
      morning,
⁶   that grow and burst into bloom,
    then dry up and die in the evening.

⁷ We are destroyed by your anger;
    we are terrified by your fury.
⁸ You place our sins before you,
    our secret sins where you can see
      them.

⁹ Our life is cut short by your anger;
    it fades away like a whisper.
¹⁰ Seventy years is all we have—
    eighty years, if we are strong;
  yet all they bring us is trouble and
      sorrow;
    life is soon over, and we are gone.

¹¹ Who has felt the full power of your
      anger?
    Who knows what fear your fury can
      bring?
¹² Teach us how short our life is,
    so that we may become wise.

¹³ How much longer will your anger last?
    Have pity, O LORD, on your servants!
¹⁴ Fill us each morning with your
      constant love,
    so that we may sing and be glad all
      our life.
¹⁵ Give us now as much happiness as the
      sadness you gave us
    during all our years of misery.

¹⁶ Let us, your servants, see your mighty
          deeds;
       let our descendants see your glorious
          might.
¹⁷ LORD our God, may your blessings be
          with us.
       Give us success in all we do!

God Our Protector

91 Whoever goes to the LORD for
          safety,
    whoever remains under the
       protection of the Almighty,
² can say to him,
       "You are my defender and protector.
       You are my God; in you I trust."
³ He will keep you safe from all hidden
          dangers
       and from all deadly diseases.
⁴ He will cover you with his wings;
       you will be safe in his care;
       his faithfulness will protect and
          defend you.
⁵ You need not fear any dangers at night
       or sudden attacks during the day
⁶   or the plagues that strike in the dark
       or the evils that kill in daylight.

⁷ A thousand may fall dead beside you,
       ten thousand all around you,
       but you will not be harmed.
⁸ You will look and see
       how the wicked are punished.

⁹ You have made the LORD your^x
          defender,
       the Most High your protector,
¹⁰ and so no disaster will strike you,
       no violence will come near your
          home.

^x *Probable text* your; *Hebrew* my.

11 God will put his angels in charge of
   you
    to protect you wherever you go.
12 They will hold you up with their hands
    to keep you from hurting your feet on
    the stones.
13 You will trample down lions and
   snakes,
    fierce lions and poisonous snakes.

14 God says, "I will save those who love
   me
    and will protect those who
    acknowledge me as LORD.
15 When they call to me, I will answer
   them;
    when they are in trouble, I will be
    with them.
    I will rescue them and honor them.
16 I will reward them with long life;
    I will save them."

A Song of Praise[j]

92 How good it is to give thanks to
      you, O LORD,
    to sing in your honor, O Most High
    God,
2 to proclaim your constant love every
    morning
    and your faithfulness every night,
3 with the music of stringed instruments
    and with melody on the harp.
4 Your mighty deeds, O LORD, make me
   glad;
    because of what you have done, I
    sing for joy.

5 How great are your actions, LORD!
    How deep are your thoughts!

j HEBREW TITLE: *A psalm; a song for the Sabbath.*

⁶ This is something a fool cannot know;
  a stupid man cannot understand:
⁷ the wicked may grow like weeds,
  those who do wrong may prosper;
yet they will be totally destroyed,
⁸   because you, LORD, are supreme
      forever.

⁹ We know that your enemies will die,
  and all the wicked will be defeated.
¹⁰ You have made me as strong as a wild
    ox;
  you have blessed me with happiness
¹¹ I have seen the defeat of my enemies
  and heard the cries of the wicked.

¹² The righteous will flourish like palm
    trees;
  they will grow like the cedars of
    Lebanon.
¹³ They are like trees planted in the house
    of the LORD,
  that flourish in the Temple of our
    God,
¹⁴   that still bear fruit in old age
  and are always green and strong.
¹⁵ This shows that the LORD is just,
  that there is no wrong in my
    protector.

God the King

93 The LORD is king.
      He is clothed with majesty and
        strength.
The earth is set firmly in place
  and cannot be moved.
² Your throne, O LORD, has been firm
  from the beginning,
  and you existed before time began.

³ The ocean depths raise their voice, O
    LORD;
  they raise their voice and roar.

⁴ The LORD rules supreme in heaven,
    greater than the roar of the ocean,
    more powerful than the waves of the
        sea.

⁵ Your laws are eternal, LORD,
    and your Temple is holy indeed,
    forever and ever.

God the Judge of All

94 LORD, you are a God who
            punishes;
    reveal your anger!
² You are the judge of all men;
    rise and give the proud what they
        deserve!
³ How much longer will the wicked be
        glad?
    How much longer, LORD?
⁴ How much longer will criminals be
        proud
    and boast about their crimes?

⁵ They crush your people, LORD;
    they oppress those who belong to
        you.
⁶ They kill widows and orphans,
    and murder the strangers who live in
        our land.
⁷ They say, "The LORD does not see us;
    the God of Israel does not notice."

⁸ My people, how can you be such stupid
        fools?
    When will you ever learn?
⁹ God made our ears—can't he hear?
    He made our eyes—can't he see?
¹⁰ He scolds the nations—won't he punish
        them? ˣ
    He is the teacher of all men—hasn't
        he any knowledge?

ˣ them?; or our wicked leaders?

11 The LORD knows what they think;
   he knows how senseless their
   reasoning is.

12 LORD, how happy is the person you
      instruct,
   the one to whom you teach your law!
13 You give him rest from days of trouble
   until a pit is dug to trap the wicked.
14 The LORD will not abandon his people;
   he will not desert those who belong
      to him.
15 Justice will again be found in the
      courts,
   and all righteous people will support
      it.

16 Who stood up for me against the
      wicked?
   Who took my side against the
      evildoers?
17 If the LORD had not helped me,
   I would have gone quickly to the
      land of silence.[k]
18 I said, "I am falling";
   but your constant love, O LORD, held
      me up.
19 Whenever I am anxious and worried,
   you comfort me and make me glad.

20 You have nothing to do with corrupt
      judges,
   who make injustice legal,
21   who plot against good men
   and sentence the innocent to death.
22 But the LORD defends me;
   my God protects me.
23 He will punish them for their
      wickedness
   and destroy them for their sins;
   the LORD our God will destroy them.

[k] LAND OF SILENCE: *The world of the dead (see 6.5).*

A Song of Praise

95 Come, let us praise the LORD!
Let us sing for joy to God, who
protects us!

2 Let us come before him with
thanksgiving
and sing joyful songs of praise.

3 For the LORD is a mighty God,
a mighty king over all the gods.

4 He rules over the whole earth,
from the deepest caves to the highest
hills.

5 He rules over the sea, which he made;
the land also, which he himself
formed.

Let us praise the LORD! (95.1)

⁶ Come, let us bow down and worship
        him;
    let us kneel before the LORD, our
        Maker!
⁷ He is our God;
    we are the people he cares for,
    the flock for which he provides.

  Listen today to what he says:
⁸ "Don't be stubborn, as your ancestors
        were at Meribah,
    as they were that day in the desert at
        Massah.
⁹ There they put me to the test and tried
        me,
    although they had seen what I did for
        them.
¹⁰ For forty years I was disgusted with
        those people.
    I said, 'How disloyal they are!
    They refuse to obey my commands.'
¹¹ I was angry and made a solemn
        promise:
    'You will never enter the land
    where I would have given you rest.' "

God the Supreme King
(1 Chronicles 16.23-33)

96 Sing a new song to the LORD!
        Sing to the LORD, all the world!
² Sing to the LORD, and praise him!
    Proclaim every day the good news
        that he has saved us.
³ Proclaim his glory to the nations,
    his mighty deeds to all peoples.

⁴ The LORD is great and is to be highly
        praised;
    he is to be honored more than all the
        gods.

5 The gods of all other nations are only
        idols,
    but the LORD created the heavens.
6 Glory and majesty surround him;
    power and beauty fill his Temple.

7 Praise the LORD, all people on earth;
    praise his glory and might.
8 Praise the LORD's glorious name;
    bring an offering and come into his
        Temple.
9 Bow down before the Holy One when
        he appears;[l]
    tremble before him, all the earth!

10 Say to all the nations, "The LORD is
        king!
    The earth is set firmly in place and
        cannot be moved;
    he will judge the peoples with
        justice."
11 Be glad, earth and sky!
    Roar, sea, and every creature in you;
12   be glad, fields, and everything in you!
    The trees in the woods will shout for
        joy
13   when the LORD comes to rule the
        earth.
    He will rule the peoples of the world
        with justice and fairness.

God the Supreme Ruler

97   The LORD is king! Earth, be glad!
        Rejoice, you islands of the seas!
2 Clouds and darkness surround him;
    he rules with righteousness and
        justice.
3 Fire goes in front of him
    and burns up his enemies around
        him.

_____
[l] when he appears; or in garments of worship.

4 His lightning lights up the world;
    the earth sees it and trembles.
5 The hills melt like wax before the
        LORD,
    before the Lord of all the earth.
6 The heavens proclaim his righteousness,
    and all the nations see his glory.

7 Everyone who worships idols is put to
        shame;
    all the gods bow down[m] before the
        LORD.
8 The people of Zion are glad,
    and the cities of Judah rejoice
    because of your judgments, O LORD.
9 LORD Almighty, you are ruler of all the
        earth;
    you are much greater than all the
        gods.

10 The LORD loves those who hate evil;[n]
    he protects the lives of his people;
    he rescues them from the power of
        the wicked.
11 Light shines on the righteous,
    and gladness on the good.
12 All you that are righteous be glad
    because of what the LORD has done!
Remember what the holy God has
        done,
    and give thanks to him.

God the Ruler of the World [x]

98   Sing a new song to the LORD;
        he has done wonderful things!
By his own power and holy strength
    he has won the victory.

---

[m] all the gods bow down; *or* bow down, all gods.   [n] *Probable text*
The LORD loves those who hate evil; *Hebrew* Hate evil, you who
love the LORD.   [x] HEBREW TITLE: *A psalm.*

² The Lord announced his victory;
   he made his saving power known to
      the nations.
³ He kept his promise to the people of
      Israel
   with loyalty and constant love for
      them.
All people everywhere have seen the
      victory of our God.

⁴ Sing for joy to the Lord, all the earth;
   praise him with songs and shouts of
      joy!
⁵ Sing praises to the Lord!
   Play music on the harps!
⁶ Blow trumpets and horns,
   and shout for joy to the Lord, our
      king.

⁷ Roar, sea, and every creature in you;
   sing, earth, and all who live on you!
⁸ Clap your hands, you rivers;
   you hills, sing together with joy
      before the Lord,
⁹ because he comes to rule the earth.
He will rule the peoples of the world
   with justice and fairness.

God the Supreme King

99 The Lord is king,
      and the people tremble.
He sits on his throne above the winged
   creatures,
   and the earth shakes.
² The Lord is mighty in Zion;
   he is supreme over all the nations.
³ Everyone will praise his great and
      majestic name.
   Holy is he!

4 Mighty king,⁰ you love what is right;
    you have established justice in Israel;
    you have brought righteousness and
        fairness.
5 Praise the LORD our God;
    worship before his throne!
    Holy is he!

6 Moses and Aaron were his priests,
    and Samuel was one who prayed to
        him;
    they called to the LORD, and he
        answered them.
7 He spoke to them from the pillar of
        cloud;
    they obeyed the laws and commands
        that he gave them.

8 O LORD, our God, you answered your
        people;
    you showed them that you are a God
        who forgives,
    even though you punished them for
        their sins.
9 Praise the LORD our God,
    and worship at his sacred hill!ᵖ
    The LORD our God is holy.

A Hymn of Praise�q

100 Sing to the LORD, all the
        world!
2 Worship the LORD with joy;
    come before him with happy songs!

3 Acknowledge that the LORD is God.
    He made us, and we belong to him;
    we are his people, we are his flock.

⁰ *Probable text* Mighty king; *Hebrew* The might of the king.
ᵖ SACRED HILL: *See 2.6.*   q HEBREW TITLE: *A psalm of thanksgiving.*

⁴ Enter the Temple gates with
        thanksgiving;
    go into its courts with praise.
    Give thanks to him and praise him.

⁵ The LORD is good;
    his love is eternal
    and his faithfulness lasts forever.

A King's Promise *

101 My song is about loyalty and
              justice,
    and I sing it to you, O LORD.
² My conduct will be faultless.
    When will you come to me?

    will live a pure life in my house
³   and will never tolerate evil.
    I hate the actions of those who turn
        away from God;
    I will have nothing to do with them.
⁴ I will not be dishonest *
    and will have no dealings with evil. *
⁵ I will get rid of anyone
    who whispers evil things about
        someone else;
    I will not tolerate a man
        who is proud and arrogant.

⁶ I will approve of those who are faithful
        to God
    and will let them live in my palace.
    Those who are completely honest
        will be allowed to serve me.

⁷ No liar will live in my palace;
    no hypocrite will remain in my
        presence.

* HEBREW TITLE: *A psalm by David.*   * not be dishonest; *or* stay
away from dishonest people.   * evil; *or* evil men.

8 Day after day I will destroy
   the wicked in our land;
I will expel all evil men
   from the city of the LORD.

The Prayer of a Troubled Young Man "

102 Listen to my prayer, O LORD,
        and hear my cry for help!
2 When I am in trouble,
    don't turn away from me!
Listen to me,
    and answer me quickly when I call!

3 My life is disappearing like smoke;
    my body is burning like fire.
4 I am beaten down like dry grass;
    I have lost my desire for food.
5 I groan aloud;
    I am nothing but skin and bones.
6 I am like a wild bird in the desert,
    like an owl in abandoned ruins.
7 I lie awake;
    I am like a lonely bird on a housetop.
8 All day long my enemies insult me;
    those who mock me use my name in
        cursing.

9-10 Because of your anger and fury,
        ashes are my food,
        and my tears are mixed with my
            drink.
You picked me up and threw me away.
11 My life is like the evening shadows;
    I am like dry grass.

12 But you, O LORD, are king forever;
    all generations will remember you.

" HEBREW TITLE: *A prayer by a weary sufferer who pours out his
complaints to the LORD.*

¹³ You will rise and take pity on Zion;
  the time has come to have mercy on
    her;
  this is the right time.
¹⁴ Your servants love her,
  even though she is destroyed;
they have pity on her,
  even though she is in ruins.

¹⁵ The nations will fear the LORD;
  all the kings of the earth will fear his
    power.
¹⁶ When the LORD rebuilds Zion,
  he will reveal his greatness.
¹⁷ He will hear his abandoned people
  and listen to their prayer.

¹⁸ Write down for the coming generation
  what the LORD has done,
  so that people not yet born will
    praise him.
¹⁹ The LORD looked down from his holy
    place on high,
  he looked down from heaven to
    earth.
²⁰ He heard the groans of prisoners
  and set free those who were
    condemned to die.
²¹ And so his name will be proclaimed in
    Zion,
  and he will be praised in Jerusalem
²² when nations and kingdoms come
    together
  and worship the LORD.

²³ The LORD has made me weak while I
    am still young;
  he has shortened my life.
²⁴ O God, do not take me away now
  before I grow old.

  O LORD, you live forever;

²⁵ long ago you created the earth,
    and with your own hands you made
      the heavens.
²⁶ They will disappear, but you will
      remain;
    they will all wear out like clothes.
You will discard them like clothes,
    and they will vanish.
²⁷ But you are always the same,
    and your life never ends.
²⁸ Our children will live in safety,
    and under your protection
      their descendants will be secure.

The Love of God [v]

103 Praise the LORD, my soul!
    All my being, praise his holy
      name!
² Praise the LORD, my soul,
    and do not forget how kind he is.
³ He forgives all my sins
    and heals all my diseases.
⁴ He keeps me from the grave
    and blesses me with love and mercy.
⁵ He fills my life[w] with good things,
    so that I stay young and strong like
      an eagle.

The LORD judges in favor of the
      oppressed
    and gives them their rights.
⁷ He revealed his plans to Moses
    and let the people of Israel see his
      mighty deeds.
⁸ The LORD is merciful and loving,
    slow to become angry and full of
      constant love.
⁹ He does not keep on rebuking;
    he is not angry forever.

[v] HEBREW TITLE: *By David.*   [w] *Probable text* my life; *Hebrew unclear.*

¹⁰ He does not punish us as we deserve
    or repay us according to our sins and
       wrongs.
¹¹ As high as the sky is above the earth,
    so great is his love for those who
       have reverence for him.
¹² As far as the east is from the west,
    so far does he remove our sins from
       us.
¹³ As a father is kind to his children,
    so the LORD is kind to those who
       honor him.
¹⁴ He knows what we are made of;
    he remembers that we are dust.

The wind blows on it, and it is gone. (103.16)

¹⁵ As for us, our life is like grass.
We grow and flourish like a wild
flower;
¹⁶ then the wind blows on it, and it is
gone—
no one sees it again.
¹⁷ But for those who honor the LORD, his
love lasts forever,
and his goodness endures for all
generations
¹⁸ of those who are true to his covenant
and who faithfully obey his
commands.

¹⁹ The LORD placed his throne in heaven;
he is king over all.
²⁰ Praise the LORD, you strong and mighty
angels,
who obey his commands,
who listen to what he says.
²¹ Praise the LORD, all you heavenly
powers,
you servants of his, who do his will!
²² Praise the LORD, all his creatures
in all the places he rules.
Praise the LORD, my soul!

In Praise of the Creator

104   Praise the LORD, my soul!
O LORD, my God, how great
you are!
You are clothed with majesty and glory;
²   you cover yourself with light.
You spread out the heavens like a tent
³   and built your home on the waters
above.ˣ
You use the clouds as your chariot
and ride on the wings of the wind.

ˣ THE WATERS ABOVE: *A reference to the waters above the celestial
dome (Genesis 1.6-7).*

4 You use the winds as your messengers
    and flashes of lightning as your
      servants.

5 You have set the earth firmly on its
      foundations,
    and it will never be moved.
6 You placed the ocean over it like a
      robe,
    and the water covered the mountains.
7 When you rebuked the waters, they
      fled;
    they rushed away when they heard
      your shout of command.
8 They flowed over the mountains and
      into the valleys,
    to the place you had made for them.
9 You set a boundary they can never
      pass,
    to keep them from covering the earth
      again.

10 You make springs flow in the valleys,
    and rivers run between the hills.
11 They provide water for the wild
      animals;
    there the wild donkeys quench their
      thirst.
12 In the trees near by,
    the birds make their nests and sing.

13 From the sky you send rain on the hills,
    and the earth is filled with your
      blessings.
14 You make grass grow for the cattle
    and plants for man to use,
  so that he can grow his crops
15   and produce wine to make him
      happy,
    olive oil to make him cheerful,
    and bread to give him strength.

You make springs flow in the valleys. (104.10)

¹⁶ The cedars of Lebanon get plenty of
  rain—
    the LORD's own trees, which he
    planted.
¹⁷ There the birds build their nests;
    the storks nest in the fir trees.
¹⁸ The wild goats live in the high
  mountains,
    and the rock badgers hide in the
    cliffs.

¹⁹ You created the moon to mark the
  months;
    the sun knows the time to set.
²⁰ You made the night, and in the
  darkness
    all the wild animals come out.
²¹ The young lions roar while they hunt,
    looking for the food that God
    provides.
²² When the sun rises, they go back
    and lie down in their dens.
²³ Then people go out to do their work
    and keep working until evening.

²⁴ LORD, you have made so many things!
    How wisely you made them all!
    The earth is filled with your
    creatures.
²⁵ There is the ocean, large and wide,
    where countless creatures live,
    large and small alike.
²⁶ The ships sail on it, and in it plays
  Leviathan,
    that sea monster which you made.ʸ

²⁷ All of them depend on you
    to give them food when they need it.
²⁸ You give it to them, and they eat it;
    you provide food, and they are
    satisfied.

ʸ in it plays . . . made; *or* Leviathan is there, that sea monster you
made to amuse you.

29 When you turn away, they are afraid;
    when you take away your breath,
        they die
    and go back to the dust from which
        they came.
30 But when you give them breath,[2] they
    are created;
    you give new life to the earth.

31 May the glory of the LORD last forever!
    May the LORD be happy with what
        he has made!
32 He looks at the earth, and it trembles;
    he touches the mountains, and they
        pour out smoke.

33 I will sing to the LORD all my life;
    as long as I live I will sing praises to
        my God.
34 May he be pleased with my song,
    for my gladness comes from him.
35 May sinners be destroyed from the
    earth;
    may the wicked be no more.

Praise the LORD, my soul!
Praise the LORD!

God and His People
(1 Chronicles 16.8-22)

105 Give thanks to the LORD,
        proclaim his greatness;
    tell the nations what he has done.
2 Sing praise to the LORD;
    tell the wonderful things he has done.
3 Be glad that we belong to him;
    let all who worship him rejoice.
4 Go to the LORD for help;
    and worship him continually.

---

[2] give them breath; or send out your spirit.

5-6 You descendants of Abraham, his
        servant;
    you descendants of Jacob, the man he
        chose:
  remember the miracles that God
        performed
    and the judgments that he gave.

7 The LORD is our God;
    his commands are for all the world.
8 He will keep his covenant forever,
    his promises for a thousand
        generations.
9 He will keep the agreement he made
        with Abraham
    and his promise to Isaac.
10 The LORD made a covenant with Jacob,
    one that will last forever.
11 "I will give you the land of Canaan," he
        said.
    "It will be your own possession."

12 God's people were few in number,
    strangers in the land of Canaan.
13 They wandered from country to
        country,
    from one kingdom to another.
14 But God let no one oppress them;
    to protect them, he warned the kings:
15 "Don't harm my chosen servants;
    do not touch my prophets."

16 The LORD sent famine to their country
    and took away all their food.
17 But he sent a man ahead of them,
    Joseph, who had been sold as a slave.
18 His feet were kept in chains,
    and an iron collar was around his
        neck,
19   until what he had predicted came
        true.
  The word of the LORD proved him
        right.

²⁰ Then the king of Egypt had him
    released;
    the ruler of nations set him free.
²¹ He put him in charge of his government
    and made him ruler over all the land,
²²   with power over the king's officials
    and authority to instruct his advisers.

²³ Then Jacob went to Egypt
    and settled in that country.
²⁴ The LORD gave many children to his
    people
    and made them stronger than their
    enemies.
²⁵ He made the Egyptians hate his people
    and treat his servants with deceit.

²⁶ Then he sent his servant Moses,
    and Aaron, whom he had chosen.
²⁷ They did God's mighty acts
    and performed miracles in Egypt.
²⁸ God sent darkness on the country,
    but the Egyptians did not obey[a] his
    command.
²⁹ He turned their rivers into blood
    and killed all their fish.
³⁰ Their country was overrun with frogs;
    even the palace was filled with them.
³¹ God commanded, and flies and gnats
    swarmed throughout the whole
    country.
³² He sent hail and lightning on their land
    instead of rain;
³³ he destroyed their grapevines and fig
    trees
    and broke down all the trees.
³⁴ He commanded, and the locusts came,
    countless millions of them;
³⁵ they ate all the plants in the land;
    they ate all the crops.

[a] *Some ancient translations* did not obey; *Hebrew* obeyed.

³⁶ He killed the first-born sons
   of all the families of Egypt.

³⁷ Then he led the Israelites out;
   they carried silver and gold,
   and all of them were healthy and
      strong.
³⁸ The Egyptians were afraid of them
   and were glad when they left.
³⁹ God put a cloud over his people
   and a fire at night to give them light.
⁴⁰ They ᵇ asked, and he sent quails;
   he gave them food from heaven to
      satisfy them.
⁴¹ He opened a rock, and water gushed
      out,
   flowing through the desert like a
      river.
⁴² He remembered his sacred promise
   to Abraham his servant.

⁴³ So he led his chosen people out,
   and they sang and shouted for joy.
⁴⁴ He gave them the lands of other
      peoples
   and let them take over their fields,
⁴⁵ so that his people would obey his laws
   and keep all his commands.

   Praise the LORD!

The LORD's Goodness to His People

106   Praise the LORD!

Give thanks to the LORD, because he is
      good;
   his love is eternal.
² Who can tell all the great things he has
      done?
   Who can praise him enough?

ᵇ *Some ancient translations* They; *Hebrew* He.

³ Happy are those who obey his
    commands,
  who always do what is right.

⁴ Remember me, LORD, when you help
    your people;
  include me when you save them.
⁵ Let me see the prosperity of your
    people
  and share in the happiness of your
    nation,
  in the glad pride of those who belong
    to you.

⁶ We have sinned as our ancestors did;
  we have been wicked and evil.
⁷ Our ancestors in Egypt did not
    understand God's wonderful acts;
  they forgot the many times he
    showed them his love,
  and they rebelled against the
    Almighty ᶜ at the Red Sea.
⁸ But he saved them, as he had promised,
  in order to show his great power.
⁹ He gave a command to the Red Sea,
    and it dried up;
  he led his people across on dry land.
¹⁰ He saved them from those who hated
    them;
  he rescued them from their enemies.
¹¹ But the water drowned their enemies;
  not one of them was left.
¹² Then his people believed his promises
  and sang praises to him.

¹³ But they quickly forgot what he had
    done
  and acted without waiting for his
    advice.

ᶜ *Probable text* the Almighty; *Hebrew* the sea.

14 They were filled with craving in the
   desert
      and put God to the test;
15 so he gave them what they asked for,
      but also sent a terrible disease among
      them.

16 There in the desert they were jealous of
      Moses
      and of Aaron, the LORD's holy
      servant.
17 Then the earth opened up and
      swallowed Dathan
      and buried Abiram and his family;
18 fire came down on their followers
      and burned up those wicked people.

19 They made a gold bull-calf at Sinai
      and worshiped that idol;
20 they exchanged the glory of God
      for the image of an animal that eats
      grass.
21 They forgot the God who had saved
      them
      by his mighty acts in Egypt.
22 What wonderful things he did there!
      What amazing things at the Red Sea!
23 When God said that he would destroy
      his people,
      his chosen servant, Moses, stood up
      against God
      and kept his anger from destroying
      them.

24 Then they rejected the pleasant land,
      because they did not believe God's
      promise.
25 They stayed in their tents and grumbled
      and would not listen to the LORD.
26 So he gave them a solemn warning
      that he would make them die in the
      desert

²⁷ and scatter their descendants among
    the heathen,
letting them die in foreign countries.

²⁸ Then at Peor, God's people joined in
    the worship of Baal
and ate sacrifices offered to dead
    gods.
²⁹ They stirred up the LORD's anger by
    their actions,
and a terrible disease broke out
    among them.
³⁰ But Phinehas stood up and punished
    the guilty,
and the plague was stopped.
³¹ This has been remembered in his favor
    ever since
and will be for all time to come.

³² At the springs of Meribah the people
    made the LORD angry,
and Moses was in trouble on their
    account.
³³ They made him so bitter
that he spoke without stopping to
    think.

³⁴ They did not kill the heathen,
    as the LORD had commanded them to
    do,
³⁵ but they intermarried with them
and adopted their pagan ways.
³⁶ God's people worshiped idols,
and this caused their destruction.
³⁷ They offered their own sons and
    daughters
as sacrifices to the idols of Canaan.
³⁸ They killed those innocent children,
and the land was defiled by those
    murders.
³⁹ They made themselves impure by their
    actions
and were unfaithful to God.

⁴⁰ So the LORD was angry with his people;
      he was disgusted with them.
⁴¹ He abandoned them to the power of the
            heathen,
      and their enemies ruled over them.
⁴² They were oppressed by their enemies
      and were in complete subjection to
            them.
⁴³ Many times the LORD rescued his
            people,
      but they chose to rebel against him
      and sank deeper into sin.
⁴⁴ Yet the LORD heard them when they
            cried out,
      and he took notice of their distress.
⁴⁵ For their sake he remembered his
            covenant,
      and because of his great love he
            relented.
⁴⁶ He made all their oppressors
      feel sorry for them.

⁴⁷ Save us, O LORD our God,
      and bring us back from among the
            nations,
   so that we may be thankful
      and praise your holy name.

⁴⁸ Praise the LORD, the God of Israel,
      praise him now and forever!
      Let everyone say, "Amen!"

                  Praise the LORD!

BOOK FIVE
(Psalms 107—150)

In Praise of God's Goodness

107   "Give thanks to the LORD,
            because he is good;
   his love is eternal!"

2 Repeat these words in praise to the
LORD,
   all you whom he has saved.
He has rescued you from your enemies
3   and has brought you back from
     foreign countries,
   from east and west, from north and
     south.^d

4 Some wandered in the trackless desert
   and could not find their way to a city
     to live in.
5 They were hungry and thirsty
   and had given up all hope.
6 Then in their trouble they called to the
LORD,
   and he saved them from their distress.
7 He led them by a straight road
   to a city where they could live.
8 They must thank the LORD for his
    constant love,
   for the wonderful things he did for
    them.
9 He satisfies those who are thirsty
   and fills the hungry with good things.

10 Some were living in gloom and
    darkness,
   prisoners suffering in chains,
11 because they had rebelled against the
    commands of Almighty God
   and had rejected his instructions.
12 They were worn out from hard work;
   they would fall down, and no one
    would help.
13 Then in their trouble they called to the
LORD,
   and he saved them from their distress.

^d *Probable text* south: *Hebrew* the Mediterranean Sea *(meaning "west")*.

¹⁴ He brought them out of their gloom
      and darkness
   and broke their chains in pieces.
¹⁵ They must thank the LORD for his
      constant love,
   for the wonderful things he did for
      them.
¹⁶ He breaks down doors of bronze
   and smashes iron bars.

¹⁷ Some were fools, suffering because of
      their sins
   and because of their evil;
¹⁸ they couldn't stand the sight of food
   and were close to death.
¹⁹ Then in their trouble they called to the
      LORD,
   and he saved them from their distress.
²⁰ He healed them with his command
   and saved them from the grave.
²¹ They must thank the LORD for his
      constant love,
   for the wonderful things he did for
      them.
²² They must thank him with sacrifices,
   and with songs of joy must tell all
      that he has done.

²³ Some sailed over the ocean in ships,
   earning their living on the seas.
²⁴ They saw what the LORD can do,
   his wonderful acts on the seas.
²⁵ He commanded, and a mighty wind
      began to blow
   and stirred up the waves.
²⁶ The ships were lifted high in the air
   and plunged down into the depths.
  In such danger the men lost their
      courage;
²⁷   they stumbled and staggered like
      drunks—
   all their skill was useless.

²⁸ Then in their trouble they called to the
  LORD,
  and he saved them from their distress.
²⁹ He calmed the raging storm,
  and the waves became quiet.
³⁰ They were glad because of the calm,
  and he brought them safe to the port
  they wanted.

And he brought them safe to the port. (107.30)

³¹ They must thank the LORD for his
  constant love,
  for the wonderful things he did for
  them.
³² They must proclaim his greatness in the
  assembly of the people
  and praise him before the council of
  the leaders.

³³ The LORD made rivers dry up
  completely
  and stopped springs from flowing.
³⁴ He made rich soil become a salty
  wasteland
  because of the wickedness of those
  who lived there.

35 He changed deserts into pools of water
   and dry land into flowing springs.
36 He let hungry people settle there,
   and they built a city to live in.
37 They sowed the fields and planted
      grapevines
   and reaped an abundant harvest.
38 He blessed his people, and they had
      many children;
   he kept their herds of cattle from
      decreasing.

39 When God's people were defeated and
      humiliated
   by cruel oppression and suffering,
40 he showed contempt for their
      oppressors
   and made them wander in trackless
      deserts.
41 But he rescued the needy from their
      misery
   and made their families increase like
      flocks.
42 The righteous see this and are glad,
   but all the wicked are put to silence.

43 May those who are wise think about
      these things;
   may they consider the LORD's
      constant love.

A Prayer for Help against Enemies[f]
(Psalms 57.7-11; 60.5-12)

108 I have complete confidence, O
         God!
   I will sing and praise you!
   Wake up, my soul!
2   Wake up, my harp and lyre!
   I will wake up the sun.

[f] HEBREW TITLE: *A psalm by David; a song.*

3 I will thank you, O LORD, among the
    nations.
    I will praise you among the peoples.
4 Your constant love reaches above the
    heavens;
    your faithfulness touches the skies.

5 Show your greatness in the sky, O God,
    and your glory over all the earth.
6 Save us by your might; answer my
    prayer,
    so that the people you love may be
    rescued.

7 From his sanctuary[g] God has said,
    "In triumph I will divide Shechem
    and distribute Sukkoth Valley to my
    people.
8 Gilead is mine, and Manasseh too;
    Ephraim is my helmet
    and Judah my royal scepter.
9 But I will use Moab as my washbowl,
    and I will throw my sandals on
    Edom,
    as a sign that I own it.
    I will shout in triumph over the
    Philistines."

10 Who, O God, will take me into the
    fortified city?
    Who will lead me to Edom?
11 Have you really rejected us?
    Aren't you going to march out with
    our armies?
12 Help us against the enemy;
    human help is worthless.
13 With God on our side we will win;
    he will defeat our enemies.

g From his sanctuary; or In his holiness.

The Complaint of a Man in Trouble [h]

109

I praise you, God; don't remain silent!

2 Wicked men and liars have attacked me.
They tell lies about me,

3   and they say evil things about me,
attacking me for no reason.

4 They oppose me, even though I love them
and have prayed for them. [i]

5 They pay me back evil for good
and hatred for love.

6 Choose some corrupt judge to try my enemy,
and let one of his own enemies accuse him.

7 May he be tried and found guilty;
may even his prayer be considered a crime!

8 May his life soon be ended;
may another man take his job!

9 May his children become orphans,
and his wife a widow!

10 May his children be homeless beggars;
may they be driven from [j] the ruins they live in!

11 May his creditors take away all his property,
and may strangers get everything he worked for.

12 May no one ever be kind to him
or care for the orphans he leaves behind.

13 May all his descendants die,
and may his name be forgotten in the next generation.

---

[h] HEBREW TITLE: *A psalm by David.*   [i] *Probable text* have prayed for them; *Hebrew unclear.*   [j] *One ancient translation* be driven from; *Hebrew* seek.

14 May the LORD remember the evil of his
  ancestors
  and never forgive his mother's sins.
15 May the LORD always remember their
  sins,
  but may they themselves be
  completely forgotten!

16 That man never thought of being kind;
  he persecuted and killed
  the poor, the needy, and the helpless.
17 He loved to curse—may he be cursed!
  He hated to give blessings—may no
  one bless him!
18 He cursed as naturally as he dressed
  himself;
  may his own curses soak into his
  body like water
  and into his bones like oil!
19 May they cover him like clothes
  and always be around him like a belt!

20 LORD, punish my enemies in that
  way—
  those who say such evil things against
  me!
21 But my Sovereign LORD, help me as
  you have promised,
  and rescue me because of the
  goodness of your love.
22 I am poor and needy;
  I am hurt to the depths of my heart.
23 Like an evening shadow I am about to
  vanish;
  I am blown away like an insect.
24 My knees are weak from lack of food;
  I am nothing but skin and bones.
25 When people see me, they laugh at me;
  they shake their heads in scorn.

26 Help me, O LORD my God;
  because of your constant love, save
  me!

²⁷ Make my enemies know
   that you are the one who saves me.
²⁸ They may curse me, but you will bless
      me.
   May my persecutors be defeated,ᵏ
   and may I, your servant, be glad.
²⁹ May my enemies be covered with
      disgrace;
   may they wear their shame like a
      robe.

³⁰ I will give loud thanks to the LORD;
   I will praise him in the assembly of
      the people,
³¹ because he defends the poor man
   and saves him from those who
      condemn him to death.

The LORD and His Chosen Kingˡ

110 The LORD said to my lord, the
      king,
   "Sit here at my right side
   until I put your enemies under your
      feet."
² From Zion the LORD will extend your
      royal power.
   "Rule over your enemies," he says.
³ On the day you fight your enemies,
   your people will volunteer.
Like the dew of early morning
   your young men will come to you on
      the sacred hills.ᵐ

⁴ The LORD made a solemn promise and
      will not take it back:
   "You will be a priest forever
   in the priestly order of
      Melchizedek."ⁿ

ᵏ One ancient translation May my persecutors be defeated; Hebrew
They persecuted me and were defeated.   ˡ HEBREW TITLE: A psalm
by David.   ᵐ Verse 3 in Hebrew is unclear.   ⁿ in the priestly order
of Melchizedek; or like Melchizedek; or in the line of succession to
Melchizedek.

⁵ The Lord is at your right side;
    when he becomes angry, he will
      defeat kings.
⁶ He will pass judgment on the nations
    and fill the battlefield with corpses;
    he will defeat kings all over the earth.
⁷ The king will drink from the stream by
      the road,
    and strengthened, he will stand
      victorious.

In Praise of the LORD

111   Praise the LORD!

With all my heart I will thank the
    LORD
    in the assembly of his people.
² How wonderful are the things the LORD
      does!
    All who are delighted with them
      want to understand them.
³ All he does is full of honor and majesty;
    his righteousness is eternal.

⁴ The LORD does not let us forget his
      wonderful actions;
    he is kind and merciful.
⁵ He provides food for those who have
      reverence for him;
    he never forgets his covenant.
⁶ He has shown his power to his people
    by giving them the lands of
      foreigners.

⁷ In all he does he is faithful and just;
    all his commands are dependable.
⁸ They last for all time;
    they were given in truth and
      righteousness.

⁹ He set his people free
   and made an eternal covenant with
      them.
   Holy and mighty is he!
¹⁰ The way to become wise is to have
   reverence for the LORD;ᵃ
   he gives sound judgment to all who
      obey his commands.
   He is to be praised forever.

The Happiness of a Good Person

112   Praise the LORD!

Happy is the person who has reverence
   for the LORD,
   who takes pleasure in obeying his
      commands.
² The good man's children will be
      powerful in the land;
   his descendants will be blessed.
³ His family will be wealthy and rich,
   and he will be prosperous forever.

⁴ Light shines in the darkness for good
      men,
   for those who are merciful, kind, and
      just.
⁵ Happy is the person who is generous
      with his loans,
   who runs his business honestly.
⁶ A good person will never fail;
   he will always be remembered.

⁷ He is not afraid of receiving bad news;
   his faith is strong, and he trusts in the
      LORD.
⁸ He is not worried or afraid;
   he is certain to see his enemies
      defeated.

ᵃ The way . . . the LORD; or The most important part of wisdom is
having reverence for the LORD.

⁹ He gives generously to the needy,
   and his kindness never fails;
   he will be powerful and respected.
¹⁰ The wicked see this and are angry;
   they glare in hate and disappear;
   their hopes are gone forever.

In Praise of the LORD's Goodness

113   Praise the LORD!

You servants of the LORD,
   praise his name!
² May his name be praised,
   now and forever.
³ From the east to the west
   praise the name of the LORD!
⁴ The LORD rules over all nations;
   his glory is above the heavens.

⁵ There is no one like the LORD our God.
He lives in the heights above,
⁶   but he bends down
   to see the heavens and the earth.
⁷ He raises the poor from the dust;
   he lifts the needy from their misery
⁸ and makes them companions of princes,
   the princes of his people.
⁹ He honors the childless wife in her
      home;
   he makes her happy by giving her
      children.

Praise the LORD!

A Passover Song

114   When the people of Israel left
            Egypt,
   when Jacob's descendants left that
      foreign land,
² Judah became the Lord's holy people,
   Israel became his own possession.

³ The Red Sea looked and ran away;
  the Jordan River stopped flowing.
⁴ The mountains skipped like goats;
  the hills jumped around like lambs.

⁵ What happened, Sea, to make you run
    away?
  And you, O Jordan, why did you stop
    flowing?
⁶ You mountains, why did you skip like
    goats?
  You hills, why did you jump around
    like lambs?

⁷ Tremble, earth, at the Lord's coming,
  at the presence of the God of Jacob,
⁸ who changes rocks into pools of water
  and solid cliffs into flowing springs.

The One True God

115 To you alone, O Lord, to you
    alone,
  and not to us, must glory be given
  because of your constant love and
    faithfulness.

² Why should the nations ask us,
  "Where is your God?"
³ Our God is in heaven;
  he does whatever he wishes.
⁴ Their gods are made of silver and gold,
  formed by human hands.
⁵ They have mouths, but cannot speak,
  and eyes, but cannot see.
⁶ They have ears, but cannot hear,
  and noses, but cannot smell.
⁷ They have hands, but cannot feel,
  and feet, but cannot walk;
  they cannot make a sound.

8 May all who made them and who trust
in them
become[p] like the idols they have
made.

9 Trust in the LORD, you people of Israel.
He helps you and protects you.
10 Trust in the LORD, you priests of God.
He helps you and protects you.
11 Trust in the LORD, all you that worship
him.
He helps you and protects you.

12 The LORD remembers us and will bless
us;
he will bless the people of Israel
and all the priests of God.
13 He will bless everyone who honors
him,
the great and the small alike.

14 May the LORD give you children—
you and your descendants!
15 May you be blessed by the LORD,
who made heaven and earth!

16 Heaven belongs to the LORD alone,
but he gave the earth to man.
17 The LORD is not praised by the dead,
by any who go down to the land of
silence.[q]
18 But we, the living, will give thanks to
him
now and forever.

Praise the LORD!

[p] May all . . . become; or All who made them and who trust in
them will become.   [q] LAND OF SILENCE: The world of the dead (see
6.5).

A Man Saved from Death Praises God

116 I love the LORD, because he
hears me;
he listens to my prayers.
2 He listens to me
every time I call to him.
3 The danger of death was all around me;
the horrors of the grave closed in on
me;
I was filled with fear and anxiety.
4 Then I called to the LORD,
"I beg you, LORD, save me!"

5 The LORD is merciful and good;
our God is compassionate.
6 The LORD protects the helpless;
when I was in danger, he saved me.
7 Be confident, my heart,
because the LORD has been good to
me.

8 The LORD saved me from death;
he stopped my tears
and kept me from defeat.
9 And so I walk in the presence of the
LORD
in the world of the living.
10 I kept on believing, even when I said,
"I am completely crushed,"
11 even when I was afraid and said,
"No one can be trusted."

12 What can I offer the LORD
for all his goodness to me?
13 I will bring a wine offering to the
LORD,
to thank him for saving me.
14 In the assembly of all his people
I will give him what I have promised.

15 How painful it is to the LORD
when one of his people dies!

¹⁶ I am your servant, LORD;
    I serve you just as my mother did.
You have saved me from death.
¹⁷ I will give you a sacrifice of
      thanksgiving
    and offer my prayer to you.
¹⁸⁻¹⁹ In the assembly of all your people,
    in the sanctuary of your Temple in
      Jerusalem,
    I will give you what I have promised.

Praise the LORD!

In Praise of the LORD

117 Praise the LORD, all nations!
      Praise him, all peoples!
² His love for us is strong,
    and his faithfulness is eternal.

Praise the LORD!

A Prayer of Thanks for Victory

118 Give thanks to the LORD,
      because he is good,
and his love is eternal.
² Let the people of Israel say,
    "His love is eternal."
³ Let the priests of God say,
    "His love is eternal."
⁴ Let all who worship him say,
    "His love is eternal."

⁵ In my distress I called to the LORD;
    he answered me and set me free.
⁶ The LORD is with me, I will not be
      afraid;
    what can anyone do to me?
⁷ It is the LORD who helps me,
    and I will see my enemies defeated.

⁸ It is better to trust in the LORD
    than to depend on man.
⁹ It is better to trust in the LORD
    than to depend on human leaders.

¹⁰ Many enemies were around me;
    but I destroyed them by the power of
        the LORD!
¹¹ They were around me on every side;
    but I destroyed them by the power of
        the LORD!
¹² They swarmed around me like bees,
    but they burned out as quickly as a
        brush fire;
    by the power of the LORD I destroyed
        them.
¹³ I was fiercely attacked and was being
        defeated,
    but the LORD helped me.
¹⁴ The LORD makes me powerful and
        strong;
    he has saved me.

¹⁵ Listen to the glad shouts of victory in
        the tents of God's people:
    "The LORD's mighty power has done
        it!
¹⁶   His power has brought us victory—
    his mighty power in battle!"

¹⁷ I will not die; instead, I will live
    and proclaim what the LORD has
        done.
¹⁸ He has punished me severely,
    but he has not let me die.

¹⁹ Open to me the gates of the Temple;
    I will go in and give thanks to the
        LORD!

²⁰ This is the gate of the LORD;
    only the righteous can come in.

²¹ I praise you, LORD, because you heard
      me,
   because you have given me victory.

²² The stone which the builders rejected as
      worthless
   turned out to be the most important
      of all.
²³ This was done by the LORD;
   what a wonderful sight it is!
²⁴ This is the day of the LORD's victory;
   let us be happy, let us celebrate!
²⁵ Save us, LORD, save us!
   Give us success, O LORD!

We bless you. (118.26)

²⁶ May God bless the one who comes in
      the name of the LORD!
   From the Temple of the LORD we
      bless you.

27 The LORD is God; he has been good to
us.
With branches in your hands, start the
festival
and march around the altar.

28 You are my God, and I give you
thanks;
I will proclaim your greatness.

29 Give thanks to the LORD, because he is
good,
and his love is eternal.

The Law of the LORD

119

Happy are those whose lives
are faultless,
who live according to the law of the
LORD.
2 Happy are those who follow his
commands,
who obey him with all their heart.
3 They never do wrong;
they walk in the LORD's ways.
4 LORD, you have given us your laws
and told us to obey them faithfully.
5 How I hope that I shall be faithful
in keeping your instructions!
6 If I pay attention to all your commands,
then I will not be put to shame.
7 As I learn your righteous judgments,
I will praise you with a pure heart.
8 I will obey your laws;
never abandon me!

Obedience to the Law of the LORD

9 How can a young man keep his life
pure?
By obeying your commands.

¹⁰ With all my heart I try to serve you;
    keep me from disobeying your
      commandments.
¹¹ I keep your law in my heart,
    so that I will not sin against you.
¹² I praise you, O LORD;
    teach me your ways.
¹³ I will repeat aloud
    all the laws you have given.
¹⁴ I delight in following your commands
    more than in having great wealth.
¹⁵ I study your instructions;
    I examine your teachings.
¹⁶ I take pleasure in your laws;
    your commands I will not forget.

Happiness in the Law of the LORD

¹⁷ Be good to me, your servant,
    so that I may live and obey your
      teachings.
¹⁸ Open my eyes, so that I may see
    the wonderful truths in your law.
¹⁹ I am here on earth for just a little
      while;
    do not hide your commands from me.
²⁰ My heart aches with longing;
    I want to know your judgments at all
      times.
²¹ You reprimand the proud;
    cursed are those who disobey your
      commands.
²² Free me from their insults and scorn,
    because I have kept your laws.
²³ The rulers meet and plot against me,
    but I will study your teachings.
²⁴ Your instructions give me pleasure;
    they are my advisers.

Determination to Obey the Law of the LORD

²⁵ I lie defeated in the dust;
    revive me, as you have promised.

²⁶ I confessed all I have done, and you
    answered me;
  teach me your ways.
²⁷ Help me to understand your laws,
  and I will meditate on your
    wonderful teachings.ʳ
²⁸ I am overcome by sorrow;
  strengthen me, as you have promised.
²⁹ Keep me from going the wrong way,
  and in your goodness teach me your
    law.
³⁰ I have chosen to be obedient;
  I have paid attention to your
    judgments.
³¹ I have followed your instructions,
    Lord;
  don't let me be put to shame.
³² I will eagerly obey your commands,
  because you will give me more
    understanding.

A Prayer for Understanding

³³ Teach me, Lord, the meaning of your
    laws,
  and I will obey them at all times.
³⁴ Explain your law to me, and I will obey
    it;
  I will keep it with all my heart.
³⁵ Keep me obedient to your
    commandments,
  because in them I find happiness.
³⁶ Give me the desire to obey your laws
  rather than to get rich.
³⁷ Keep me from paying attention to what
    is worthless;
  be good to me, as you have promised.
³⁸ Keep your promise to me, your
    servant—
  the promise you make to those who
    obey you.

ʳ teachings; *or* deeds.

³⁹ Save me from the insults I fear;
     how wonderful are your judgments!
⁴⁰ I want to obey your commands;
     give me new life, for you are
         righteous.

Trusting the Law of the LORD

⁴¹ Show me how much you love me,
         LORD,
     and save me according to your
         promise.
⁴² Then I can answer those who insult me
     because I trust in your word.
⁴³ Enable me to speak the truth at all
         times,
     because my hope is in your
         judgments.
⁴⁴ I will always obey your law,
     forever and ever.
⁴⁵ I will live in perfect freedom,
     because I try to obey your teachings.
⁴⁶ I will announce your commands to
         kings
     and I will not be ashamed.
⁴⁷ I find pleasure in obeying your
         commands,
     because I love them.
⁴⁸ I respect and love your commandments;
     I will meditate on your instructions.

Confidence in the Law of the LORD

⁴⁹ Remember your promise to me, your
         servant;
     it has given me hope.
⁵⁰ Even in my suffering I was comforted
     because your promise gave me life.
⁵¹ The proud are always scornful of me,
     but I have not departed from your
         law.

⁵² I remember your judgments of long ago,
  and they bring me comfort, O LORD.
⁵³ When I see the wicked breaking your
    law,
  I am filled with anger.
⁵⁴ During my brief earthly life
  I compose songs about your
    commands.
⁵⁵ In the night I remember you, LORD,
  and I think about your law.
⁵⁶ I find my happiness
  in obeying your commands.

Devotion to the Law of the LORD

⁵⁷ You are all I want, O LORD;
  I promise to obey your laws.
⁵⁸ I ask you with all my heart
  to have mercy on me, as you have
    promised!
⁵⁹ I have considered my conduct,
  and I promise to follow your
    instructions.
⁶⁰ Without delay I hurry
  to obey your commands.
⁶¹ The wicked have laid a trap for me,
  but I do not forget your law.
⁶² In the middle of the night I wake up
  to praise you for your righteous
    judgments.
⁶³ I am a friend of all who serve you,
  of all who obey your laws.
⁶⁴ LORD, the earth is full of your constant
    love;
  teach me your commandments.

The Value of the Law of the LORD

⁶⁵ You have kept your promise, LORD,
  and you are good to me, your
    servant.

66 Give me wisdom and knowledge,
    because I trust in your commands.
67 Before you punished me, I used to go
        wrong,
    but now I obey your word.
68 How good you are—how kind!
    Teach me your commands.
69 Proud men have told lies about me,
    but with all my heart I obey your
        instructions.
70 These men have no understanding,
    but I find pleasure in your law.
71 My punishment was good for me,
    because it made me learn your
        commands.
72 The law that you gave means more to
        me
    than all the money in the world.

The Justice of the Law of the LORD

73 You created me, and you keep me safe;
    give me understanding, so that I may
        learn your laws.
74 Those who have reverence for you will
        be glad when they see me,
    because I trust in your promise.
75 I know that your judgments are
        righteous, LORD,
    and that you punished me because
        you are faithful.
76 Let your constant love comfort me,
    as you have promised me, your
        servant.
77 Have mercy on me, and I will live
    because I take pleasure in your law.
78 May the proud be ashamed for falsely
        accusing me;
    as for me, I will meditate on your
        instructions.
79 May those who have reverence for you
        come to me—
    all those who know your commands.

⁸⁰ May I perfectly obey your
    commandments
    and be spared the shame of defeat.

A Prayer for Deliverance

⁸¹ I am worn out, LORD, waiting for you
    to save me;
    I place my trust in your word.
⁸² My eyes are tired from watching for
    what you promised,
    while I ask, "When will you help
    me?"
⁸³ I am as useless as a discarded wineskin;
    yet I have not forgotten your
    commands.
⁸⁴ How much longer must I wait?
    When will you punish those who
    persecute me?
⁸⁵ Proud men, who do not obey your law,
    have dug pits to trap me.
⁸⁶ Your commandments are all
    trustworthy;
    men persecute me with lies—help me!
⁸⁷ They have almost succeeded in killing
    me,
    but I have not neglected your
    commands.
⁸⁸ Because of your constant love be good
    to me,
    so that I may obey your laws.

Faith in the Law of the LORD

⁸⁹ Your word, O LORD, will last forever;
    it is eternal in heaven.
⁹⁰ Your faithfulness endures through all
    the ages;
    you have set the earth in place, and it
    remains.
⁹¹ All things remain to this day because of
    your command,
    because they are all your servants.

⁹² If your law had not been the source of
   my joy,
     I would have died from my sufferings.
⁹³ I will never neglect your instructions,
     because by them you have kept me
       alive.
⁹⁴ I am yours—save me!
     I have tried to obey your commands.
⁹⁵ Wicked men are waiting to kill me,
     but I will meditate on your laws.
⁹⁶ I have learned that everything has
   limits;
     but your commandment is perfect.

Love for the Law of the Lord

⁹⁷ How I love your law!
     I think about it all day long.
⁹⁸ Your commandment is with me all the
   time
     and makes me wiser than my
       enemies.
⁹⁹ I understand more than all my teachers,
     because I meditate on your
       instructions.
¹⁰⁰ I have greater wisdom than old men,
     because I obey your commands.
¹⁰¹ I have avoided all evil conduct,
     because I want to obey your word.
¹⁰² I have not neglected your instructions,
     because you yourself are my teacher.
¹⁰³ How sweet is the taste of your
    instructions—
     sweeter even than honey!
¹⁰⁴ I gain wisdom from your laws,
     and so I hate all bad conduct.

Light from the Law of the Lord

¹⁰⁵ Your word is a lamp to guide me
     and a light for my path.
¹⁰⁶ I will keep my solemn promise
     to obey your just instructions.

A light for my path. (119.105)

¹⁰⁷ My sufferings, LORD, are terrible
indeed;
    keep me alive, as you have promised.
¹⁰⁸ Accept my prayer of thanks, O LORD,
    and teach me your commands.
¹⁰⁹ I am always ready to risk my life;
    Iˢ have not forgotten your law.
¹¹⁰ Wicked men lay a trap for me,
    but I have not disobeyed your
commands.
¹¹¹ Your commandments are my eternal
possession;
    they are the joy of my heart.
¹¹² I have decided to obey your laws
    until the day I die.

ˢ I am always ready to risk my life; I; *or* My life is in constant
danger, but I.

Safety in the Law of the LORD

¹¹³ I hate those who are not completely
    loyal to you,
    but I love your law.

¹¹⁴ You are my defender and protector;
    I put my hope in your promise.

¹¹⁵ Go away from me, you sinful people.
    I will obey the commands of my God.

¹¹⁶ Give me strength, as you promised, and
    I shall live;
    don't let me be disappointed in my
    hope!

¹¹⁷ Hold me, and I will be safe,
    and I will always pay attention to
    your commands.

¹¹⁸ You reject everyone who disobeys your
    laws;
    their deceitful schemes are useless.

¹¹⁹ You treat all the wicked like rubbish,
    and so I love your instructions.

¹²⁰ Because of you I am afraid;
    I am filled with fear because of your
    judgments.

Obedience to the Law of the LORD

¹²¹ I have done what is right and good;
    don't abandon me to my enemies!

¹²² Promise that you will help your
    servant;
    don't let arrogant men oppress me!

¹²³ My eyes are tired from watching for
    your saving help,
    for the deliverance you promised.

¹²⁴ Treat me according to your constant
    love,
    and teach me your commands.

¹²⁵ I am your servant; give me
    understanding,
    so that I may know your teachings.

126 LORD, it is time for you to act,
    because people are disobeying your
    law.
127 I love your commands more than gold,
    more than the finest gold.
128 And so I follow all your instructions;[t]
    I hate all wrong ways.

Desire to Obey the Law of the LORD

129 Your teachings are wonderful;
    I obey them with all my heart.
130 The explanation of your teachings gives
    light
    and brings wisdom to the ignorant.
131 In my desire for your commands
    I pant with open mouth.
132 Turn to me and have mercy on me
    as you do on all those who love you.
133 As you have promised, keep me from
    falling;
    don't let me be overcome by evil.
134 Save me from those who oppress me,
    so that I may obey your commands.
135 Bless me with your presence
    and teach me your laws.
136 My tears pour down like a river,
    because people do not obey your law.

The Justice of the Law of the LORD

137 You are righteous, LORD,
    and your laws are just.
138 The rules that you have given
    are completely fair and right.
139 My anger burns in me like a fire,
    because my enemies disregard your
    commands.

[t] *Some ancient translations* all your instructions; *Hebrew unclear.*

[140] How certain your promise is!
   How I love it!
[141] I am unimportant and despised,
   but I do not neglect your teachings.
[142] Your righteousness will last forever,
   and your law is always true.
[143] I am filled with trouble and anxiety,
   but your commandments bring me
      joy.
[144] Your instructions are always just;
   give me understanding, and I shall
      live.

A Prayer for Deliverance

[145] With all my heart I call to you;
   answer me, LORD, and I will obey
      your commands!
[146] I call to you;
   save me, and I will keep your laws.
[147] Before sunrise I call to you for help;
   I place my hope in your promise.
[148] All night long I lie awake,
   to meditate on your instructions.
[149] Because your love is constant, hear me,
      O LORD;
   show your mercy, and preserve my
      life!
[150] My cruel persecutors are coming closer,
   people who never keep your law.
[151] But you are near to me, LORD,
   and all your commands are
      permanent.
[152] Long ago I learned about your
      instructions;
   you made them to last forever.

A Plea for Help

[153] Look at my suffering, and save me,
   because I have not neglected your
      law.

¹⁵⁴ Defend my cause, and set me free;
    save me, as you have promised.
¹⁵⁵ The wicked will not be saved,
    for they do not obey your laws.
¹⁵⁶ But your compassion, LORD, is great;
    show your mercy and save me!
¹⁵⁷ I have many enemies and oppressors,
    but I do not fail to obey your laws.
¹⁵⁸ When I look at those traitors, I am
        filled with disgust,
    because they do not keep your
        commands.
¹⁵⁹ See how I love your instructions, LORD.
    Your love never changes, so save me!
¹⁶⁰ The heart of your law is truth,
    and all your righteous judgments are
        eternal.

Dedication to the Law of the LORD

¹⁶¹ Powerful men attack me unjustly,
    but I respect your law.
¹⁶² How happy I am because of your
        promises—
    as happy as someone who finds rich
        treasure.
¹⁶³ I hate and detest all lies,
    but I love your law.
¹⁶⁴ Seven times each day I thank you
    for your righteous judgments.
¹⁶⁵ Those who love your law have perfect
        security,
    and there is nothing that can make
        them fall.
¹⁶⁶ I wait for you to save me, LORD,
    and I do what you command.
¹⁶⁷ I obey your teachings;
    I love them with all my heart.
¹⁶⁸ I obey your commands and your
        instructions;
    you see everything I do.

A Prayer for Help

169 Let my cry for help reach you, LORD!
   Give me understanding, as you have
      promised.
170 Listen to my prayer,
   and save me according to your
      promise!
171 I will always praise you,
   because you teach me your laws.
172 I will sing about your law,
   because your commands are just.
173 Always be ready to help me,
   because I follow your commands.
174 How I long for your saving help, O
      LORD!
   I find happiness in your law.
175 Give me life, so that I may praise you;
   may your instructions help me.
176 I wander about like a lost sheep;
   so come and look for me, your
      servant,
   because I have not neglected your
      laws.

A Prayer for Help

120 When I was in trouble, I called
      to the LORD,
   and he answered me.
2 Save me, LORD,
   from liars and deceivers.

3 You liars, what will God do to you?
   How will he punish you?
4 With a soldier's sharp arrows,
   with red-hot coals!

5 Living among you is as bad as living in
      Meshech
   or among the people of Kedar."

" MESHECH . . . KEDAR: *Two distant regions, whose people were regarded as savages.*

⁶ I have lived too long
    with people who hate peace!
⁷ When I speak of peace,
    they are for war.

The LORD Our Protector

121 I look to the mountains;
        where will my help come
        from?
² My help will come from the LORD,
    who made heaven and earth.

³ He will not let you fall;
    your protector is always awake.

⁴ The protector of Israel
    never dozes or sleeps.
⁵ The LORD will guard you;
    he is by your side to protect you.
⁶ The sun will not hurt you during the
    day,
    nor the moon during the night.

⁷ The LORD will protect you from all
    danger;
    he will keep you safe.
⁸ He will protect you as you come and go
    now and forever.

In Praise of Jerusalem ᵛ

122 I was glad when they said to
        me,
    "Let us go to the LORD's house."
² And now we are here,
    standing inside the gates of
        Jerusalem!

³ Jerusalem is a city restored
    in beautiful order and harmony.

ᵛ HEBREW TITLE: *By David.*

⁴ This is where the tribes come,
    the tribes of Israel,
  to give thanks to the Lord
    according to his command.
⁵ Here the kings of Israel
    sat to judge their people.

⁶ Pray for the peace of Jerusalem:
    "May those who love you prosper.
⁷   May there be peace inside your walls
    and safety in your palaces."
⁸ For the sake of my relatives and friends
    I say to Jerusalem, "Peace be with
      you!"
⁹ For the sake of the house of the Lord
    our God
  I pray for your prosperity.

A Prayer for Mercy

123 Lord, I look up to you,
        up to heaven, where you
          rule.
² As a servant depends on his master,
    as a maid depends on her mistress,
  so we will keep looking to you, O Lord
    our God,
      until you have mercy on us.

³ Be merciful to us, Lord, be merciful;
    we have been treated with so much
      contempt.
⁴ We have been mocked too long by the
    rich
  and scorned by proud oppressors.

God the Protector of His People ʷ

124 What if the Lord had not been
        on our side?
      Answer, O Israel!

ʷ HEBREW TITLE: *By David.*

² "If the LORD had not been on our side
  when our enemies attacked us,
³ then they would have swallowed us
  alive
  in their furious anger against us;
⁴ then the flood would have carried us
  away,
  the water would have covered us,
⁵   the raging torrent would have
  drowned us."

⁶ Let us thank the LORD,
  who has not let our enemies destroy
  us.
⁷ We have escaped like a bird from a
  hunter's trap;
  the trap is broken, and we are free!
⁸ Our help comes from the LORD,
  who made heaven and earth.

The Security of God's People

125 Those who trust in the LORD
        are like Mount Zion,
  which can never be shaken, never be
  moved.
² As the mountains surround Jerusalem,
  so the LORD surrounds his people,
  now and forever.

³ The wicked will not always rule over
  the land of the righteous;
  if they did, the righteous themselves
  might do evil.
⁴ LORD, do good to those who are good,
  to those who obey your commands.
⁵ But when you punish the wicked,
  punish also those who abandon your
  ways.

Peace be with Israel!

A Prayer for Deliverance

126 When the LORD brought us
        back to Jerusalem,ˣ
it was like a dream!

² How we laughed, how we sang for joy!
   Then the other nations said about us,
   "The LORD did great things for
       them."

³ Indeed he did great things for us;
   how happy we were!

⁴ LORD, make us prosperous again,ʸ
   just as the rain brings water back to
       dry riverbeds.

Gather the harvest with joy! (126.5)

ˣ brought us back to Jerusalem; *or* made Jerusalem prosperous
again.   ʸ make us prosperous again; *or* take us back to our land.

⁵ Let those who wept as they planted
   their crops,
   gather the harvest with joy!

⁶ Those who wept as they went out
   carrying the seed
   will come back singing for joy,
   as they bring in the harvest.

In Praise of God's Goodness[1]

127 If the LORD does not build the
          house,
   the work of the builders is useless;
   if the LORD does not protect the city,
      it does no good for the sentries to
      stand guard.
² It is useless to work so hard for a
      living,
   getting up early and going to bed late.
   For the LORD provides for those he
      loves,
      while they are asleep.

³ Children are a gift from the LORD;
   they are a real blessing.
⁴ The sons a man has when he is young
   are like arrows in a soldier's hand.
⁵ Happy is the man who has many such
      arrows.
   He will never be defeated
      when he meets his enemies in the
      place of judgment.

The Reward of Obedience to the LORD

128 Happy are those who obey the
          LORD,
   who live by his commands.

[1] HEBREW TITLE: *By Solomon.*

2 Your work will provide for your needs;
    you will be happy and prosperous.
3 Your wife will be like a fruitful vine in
    your home,
      and your sons will be like young
      olive trees around your table.
4 A man who obeys the LORD
    will surely be blessed like this.

5 May the LORD bless you from Zion!
    May you see Jerusalem prosper
    all the days of your life!
6 May you live to see your grandchildren!

Peace be with Israel!

A Prayer against Israel's Enemies

129 Israel, tell us how your
    enemies have persecuted
    you
ever since you were young.

2 "Ever since I was young,
    my enemies have persecuted me
    cruelly,
    but they have not overcome me.
3 They cut deep wounds in my back
    and made it like a plowed field.
4 But the LORD, the righteous one,
    has freed me from slavery."

5 May everyone who hates Zion
    be defeated and driven back.
6 May they all be like grass growing on
    the housetops,
    which dries up before it can grow;
7   no one gathers it up
    or carries it away in bundles.
8 No one who passes by will say,
    "May the LORD bless you!
    We bless you in the name of the
    LORD."

A Prayer for Help

130 From the depths of my despair
I call to you, LORD.

[2] Hear my cry, O Lord;
listen to my call for help!

[3] If you kept a record of our sins,
who could escape being condemned?

[4] But you forgive us,
so that we should reverently obey
you.

[5] I wait eagerly for the LORD's help,
and in his word I trust.

[6] I wait for the Lord
more eagerly than watchmen wait for
the dawn—
than watchmen wait for the dawn.

[7] Israel, trust in the LORD,
because his love is constant
and he is always willing to save.

[8] He will save his people Israel
from all their sins.

A Prayer of Humble Trust [z]

131 LORD, I have given up my
pride
and turned away from my arrogance.
I am not concerned with great matters
or with subjects too difficult for me.

[2] Instead, I am content and at peace.
As a child lies quietly in its mother's
arms,
so my heart is quiet within me.

[3] Israel, trust in the LORD
now and forever!

[z] HEBREW TITLE: *By David.*

In Praise of the Temple

132

LORD, do not forget David
and all the hardships he
endured.

2 Remember, LORD, what he promised,
the vow he made to you, the Mighty
God of Jacob:

3 "I will not go home or go to bed;
4 I will not rest or sleep,
5 until I provide a place for the LORD,
a home for the Mighty God of
Jacob."

6 In Bethlehem we heard about the
Covenant Box,
and we found it in the fields of
Jearim.
7 We said, "Let us go to the LORD's
house;
let us worship before his throne."

8 Come to the Temple, LORD, with the
Covenant Box,
the symbol of your power,
and stay here forever.
9 May your priests do always what is
right;
may your people shout for joy!

10 You made a promise to your servant
David;
do not reject your chosen king, LORD.
11 You made a solemn promise to
David—
a promise you will not take back:
"I will make one of your sons king,
and he will rule after you.
12 If your sons are true to my covenant
and to the commands I give them,
their sons, also, will succeed you for
all time as kings."

¹³ The LORD has chosen Zion;
       he wants to make it his home:
¹⁴ "This is where I will live forever;
       this is where I want to rule.
¹⁵ I will richly provide Zion with all she
           needs;
       I will satisfy her poor with food.
¹⁶ I will bless her priests in all they do,
       and her people will sing and shout
           for joy.
¹⁷ Here I will make one of David's
           descendants a great king;
       here I will preserve the rule of my
           chosen king.
¹⁸ I will cover his enemies with shame,
       but his kingdom will prosper and
           flourish."

In Praise of Brotherly Love[a]

133   How wonderful it is, how
           pleasant,
       for God's people to live together in
           harmony!
² It is like the precious anointing oil
       running down from Aaron's head and
           beard,
       down to the collar of his robes.
³ It is like the dew on Mount Hermon,
       falling on the hills of Zion.
   That is where the LORD has promised
           his blessing—
       life that never ends.

A Call to Praise God

134   Come, praise the LORD,
           all his servants,
       all who serve in his Temple at night.

[a] HEBREW TITLE: *By David.*

2 Raise your hands in prayer in the
Temple,
    and praise the LORD!

3 May the LORD, who made heaven and
earth,
    bless you from Zion!

A Hymn of Praise

135 Praise the LORD!

Praise his name, you servants of the
LORD,
2   who stand in the LORD's house,
    in the Temple of our God.
3 Praise the LORD, because he is good;
    sing praises to his name, because he
    is kind.^b
4 He chose Jacob for himself,
    the people of Israel for his own.

5 I know that our LORD is great,
    greater than all the gods.
6 He does whatever he wishes
    in heaven and on earth,
    in the seas and in the depths below.
7 He brings storm clouds from the ends
    of the earth;
    he makes lightning for the storms,
    and he brings out the wind from his
    storeroom.

8 In Egypt he killed all the first-born
    of men and animals alike.
9 There he performed miracles and
    wonders
    to punish the king and all his
    officials.
10 He destroyed many nations
    and killed powerful kings:

^b he is kind; or it is pleasant to do so.

¹¹ Sihon, king of the Amorites,
   Og, king of Bashan,
   and all the kings in Canaan.
¹² He gave their lands to his people;
   he gave them to Israel.

¹³ LORD, you will always be proclaimed as
      God;
   all generations will remember you.
¹⁴ The LORD will defend his people;
   he will take pity on his servants.

¹⁵ The gods of the nations are made of
      silver and gold;
   they are formed by human hands.
¹⁶ They have mouths, but cannot speak,
   and eyes, but cannot see.
¹⁷ They have ears, but cannot hear;
   they are not even able to breathe.
¹⁸ May all who made them and who trust
      in them
   become*c* like the idols they have
      made!

¹⁹ Praise the LORD, people of Israel;
   praise him, you priests of God!
²⁰ Praise the LORD, you Levites;
   praise him, all you that worship him!
²¹ Praise the LORD in Zion,
   in Jerusalem, his home.

   Praise the LORD!

A Hymn of Thanksgiving

136   Give thanks to the LORD,
              because he is good;
         his love is eternal.
    ² Give thanks to the greatest of all gods;
         his love is eternal.

---

c May all . . . become; *or* All who made them and who trust in
them will become.

³ Give thanks to the mightiest of all
      lords;
    his love is eternal.

⁴ He alone performs great miracles;
    his love is eternal.
⁵ By his wisdom he made the heavens;
    his love is eternal;
⁶ he built the earth on the deep waters;
    his love is eternal.
⁷ He made the sun and the moon;
    his love is eternal;
⁸ the sun to rule over the day;
    his love is eternal;
⁹ the moon and the stars to rule over the
      night;
    his love is eternal.

¹⁰ He killed the first-born sons of the
      Egyptians;
    his love is eternal.
¹¹ He led the people of Israel out of
      Egypt;
    his love is eternal;
¹² with his strong hand, his powerful arm;
    his love is eternal.
¹³ He divided the Red Sea;
    his love is eternal;
¹⁴ he led his people through it;
    his love is eternal;
¹⁵ but he drowned the king of Egypt and
      his army;
    his love is eternal.

¹⁶ He led his people through the desert;
    his love is eternal.
¹⁷ He killed powerful kings;
    his love is eternal;
¹⁸ he killed famous kings;
    his love is eternal;
¹⁹ Sihon, king of the Amorites;
    his love is eternal;

²⁰ and Og, king of Bashan;
　　his love is eternal.
²¹ He gave their lands to his people;
　　his love is eternal;
²² he gave them to Israel, his servant;
　　his love is eternal.

²³ He did not forget us when we were
　　　defeated;
　　his love is eternal;
²⁴ he freed us from our enemies;
　　his love is eternal.
²⁵ He gives food to every living creature;
　　his love is eternal.

²⁶ Give thanks to the God of heaven;
　　his love is eternal.

A Lament of Israelites in Exile

137 By the rivers of Babylon we
　　　　sat down;
　　there we wept when we remembered
　　　Zion.
² On the willows near by
　　we hung up our harps.
³ Those who captured us told us to sing;
　　they told us to entertain them:
　　"Sing us a song about Zion."

⁴ How can we sing a song to the LORD
　　in a foreign land?
⁵ May I never be able to play the harp
　　　again
　　if I forget you, Jerusalem!
⁶ May I never be able to sing again
　　if I do not remember you,
　　if I do not think of you as my greatest
　　　joy!

7 Remember, LORD, what the Edomites
        did
    the day Jerusalem was captured.
  Remember how they kept saying,
    "Tear it down to the ground!"

8 Babylon, you will be destroyed.
  Happy is the man who pays you back
    for what you have done to us—
9   who takes your babies
    and smashes them against a rock.

A Prayer of Thanksgiving[d]

138 I thank you, LORD, with all my
            heart;
      I sing praise to you before the gods.
2 I face your holy Temple,
    bow down, and praise your name
  because of your constant love and
        faithfulness,
      because you have shown that your
        name and your commands are
        supreme.[e]
3 You answered me when I called to you;
    with your strength you strengthened
        me.

4 All the kings in the world will praise
        you, LORD,
    because they have heard your
        promises.
5 They will sing about what you have
        done
    and about your great glory.
6 Even though you are so high above,
    you care for the lowly,
    and the proud cannot hide from you.

---

[d] HEBREW TITLE: *By David.* [e] *Probable text* your name and your commands are supreme; *Hebrew* your command is greater than all your name.

⁷ When I am surrounded by troubles,
  you keep me safe.
  You oppose my angry enemies
  and save me by your power.
⁸ You will do everything you have
    promised;
  LORD, your love is eternal.
  Complete the work that you have
    begun.

God's Complete Knowledge and Care *ʲ*

139 LORD, you have examined me
       and you know me.
² You know everything I do;
  from far away you understand all my
    thoughts.
³ You see me, whether I am working or
    resting;
  you know all my actions.
⁴ Even before I speak,
  you already know what I will say.
⁵ You are all around me on every side;
  you protect me with your power.
⁶ Your knowledge of me is too deep;
  it is beyond my understanding.

⁷ Where could I go to escape from you?
  Where could I get away from your
    presence?
⁸ If I went up to heaven, you would be
    there;
  if I lay down in the world of the
    dead, you would be there.
⁹ If I flew away beyond the east
  or lived in the farthest place in the
    west,
¹⁰ you would be there to lead me,
  you would be there to help me.

ʲ HEBREW TITLE: *A psalm by David.*

¹¹ I could ask the darkness to hide me
     or the light around me to turn into
          night,
¹² but even darkness is not dark for you,
     and the night is as bright as the day.
     Darkness and light are the same to
          you.

¹³ You created every part of me;
     you put me together in my mother's
          womb.
¹⁴ I praise you because you are to be
          feared;
     all you do is strange and wonderful.
     I know it with all my heart.
¹⁵ When my bones were being formed,
     carefully put together in my mother's
          womb,
     when I was growing there in secret,
     you knew that I was there—
¹⁶   you saw me before I was born.
     The days allotted to me
          had all been recorded in your book,
          before any of them ever began.
¹⁷ O God, how difficult I find your
          thoughts;ᵍ
     how many of them there are!
¹⁸ If I counted them, they would be more
          than the grains of sand.
     When I awake, I am still with you.

¹⁹ O God, how I wish you would kill the
          wicked!
     How I wish violent men would leave
          me alone!
²⁰ They say wicked things about you;
     they speak evil things against your
          name.ʰ

_____

ᵍ how difficult I find your thoughts; _or_ how precious are your
thoughts to me.   ʰ _Probable text_ they speak . . . name; _Hebrew
unclear._

²¹ O LORD, how I hate those who hate
        you!
    How I despise those who rebel
        against you!
²² I hate them with a total hatred;
    I regard them as my enemies.

²³ Examine me, O God, and know my
        mind;
    test me, and discover my thoughts.
²⁴ Find out if there is any evil in me
    and guide me in the everlasting way.ⁱ

A Prayer for Protection ʲ

140 Save me, LORD, from evil men;
        keep me safe from violent
        men.
² They are always plotting evil,
    always stirring up quarrels.
³ Their tongues are like deadly snakes;
    their words are like a cobra's poison.

⁴ Protect me, LORD, from the power of
        the wicked;
    keep me safe from violent men
    who plot my downfall.
⁵ Proud men have set a trap for me;
    they have laid their snares,
    and along the path they have set
        traps to catch me.

⁶ I say to the LORD, "You are my God."
    Hear my cry for help, LORD!
⁷ My Sovereign LORD, my strong
        defender,
    you have protected me in battle.
⁸ LORD, don't give the wicked what they
        want;
    don't let their plots succeed.

ⁱ the everlasting way; or the ways of my ancestors.   ʲ HEBREW
TITLE: A psalm by David.

9 Don't let my enemies be victorious;[k]
   make their threats against me fall
     back on them.
10 May red-hot coals fall on them;
    may they be thrown into a pit and
      never get out.
11 May those who accuse others falsely
     not succeed;
    may evil overtake violent men and
      destroy them.

12 LORD, I know that you defend the cause
     of the poor
   and the rights of the needy.
13 The righteous will praise you indeed;
    they will live in your presence.

An Evening Prayer[l]

141 I call to you, LORD; help me
        now!
    Listen to me when I call to you.
2 Receive my prayer as incense,
   my uplifted hands as an evening
     sacrifice.

3 LORD, place a guard at my mouth,
   a sentry at the door of my lips.
4 Keep me from wanting to do wrong
   and from joining evil men in their
     wickedness.
   May I never take part in their feasts.

5 A good man may punish me and rebuke
     me in kindness,
   but I will never accept honor from
     evil men,
     because I am always praying against
       their evil deeds.

---

[k] *Probable text* Don't let my enemies be victorious; *Hebrew unclear.*
[l] HEBREW TITLE: *A psalm by David.*

⁶ When their rulers are thrown down
        from rocky cliffs,
    the people will admit that my words
        were true.
⁷ Like wood that is split and chopped
        into bits,
    so their bones are scattered at the
        edge of the grave.ᵐ

⁸ But I keep trusting in you, my
        Sovereign LORD.
    I seek your protection;
        don't let me die!
⁹ Protect me from the traps they have set
        for me,
    from the snares of those evildoers.
¹⁰ May the wicked fall into their own
        traps
    while I go by unharmed.

A Prayer for Helpⁿ

142 I call to the LORD for help;
            I plead with him.
² I bring him all my complaints;
    I tell him all my troubles.
³ When I am ready to give up,
    he knows what I should do.
    In the path where I walk,
        my enemies have hidden a trap for
            me.
⁴ When I look beside me,
    I see that there is no one to help me,
        no one to protect me.
    No one cares for me.

⁵ LORD, I cry to you for help;
    you, LORD, are my protector;
    you are all I want in this life.

ᵐ *Verses 5–7 in Hebrew are unclear.*   ⁿ HEBREW TITLE: *A poem by
David, when he was in the cave; a prayer.*

⁶ Listen to my cry for help,
    for I am sunk in despair.
Save me from my enemies;
    they are too strong for me.
⁷ Set me free from my distress;ᵒ
    then in the assembly of your people I
        will praise you
    because of your goodness to me.

A Prayer for Helpᵖ

143 LORD, hear my prayer!
    In your righteousness listen to
        my plea;
    answer me in your faithfulness!
² Don't put me, your servant, on trial;
    no one is innocent in your sight.

³ My enemy has hunted me down
    and completely defeated me.
He has put me in a dark prison,
    and I am like those who died long
        ago.
⁴ So I am ready to give up;
    I am in deep despair.

⁵ I remember the days gone by;
    I think about all that you have done,
    I bring to mind all your deeds.
⁶ I lift up my hands to you in prayer;
    like dry ground my soul is thirsty for
        you.

⁷ Answer me now, LORD!
    I have lost all hope.
Don't hide yourself from me,
    or I will be among those who go
        down to the world of the dead.
⁸ Remind me each morning of your
        constant love,
    for I put my trust in you.

ᵒ distress; *or* prison.   ᵖ HEBREW TITLE: *A psalm by David.*

My prayers go up to you;
  show me the way I should go.

⁹ I go to you for protection, LORD;
  rescue me from my enemies.
¹⁰ You are my God;
  teach me to do your will.
Be good to me, and guide me on a safe
  path.

¹¹ Rescue me, LORD, as you have
  promised;
  in your goodness save me from my
  troubles!
¹² Because of your love for me, kill my
  enemies
  and destroy all my oppressors,
  for I am your servant.

A King Thanks God for Victory*a*

144 Praise the LORD, my protector!
    He trains me for battle
  and prepares me for war.
² He is my protector and defender,
  my shelter and savior,
  in whom I trust for safety.
He subdues the nations under me.

³ LORD, what is man, that you notice
  him;
  mere man, that you pay attention to
  him?
⁴ He is like a puff of wind;
  his days are like a passing shadow.

⁵ O LORD, tear the sky open and come
  down;
  touch the mountains, and they will
  pour out smoke.

a HEBREW TITLE: *By David.*

⁶ Send flashes of lightning and scatter
    your enemies;
  shoot your arrows and send them
    running.
⁷ Reach down from above,
  pull me out of the deep water, and
    rescue me;
  save me from the power of foreigners,
⁸   who never tell the truth
  and lie even under oath.

⁹ I will sing you a new song, O God;
  I will play the harp and sing to you.
¹⁰ You give victory to kings
  and rescue your servant David.
¹¹ Save me from my cruel enemies;
  rescue me from the power of
    foreigners,
  who never tell the truth
  and lie even under oath.

¹² May our sons in their youth
  be like plants that grow up strong.
  May our daughters be like stately
    columns
  which adorn the corners of a palace.
¹³ May our barns be filled
  with crops of every kind.
  May the sheep in our fields
  bear young by the tens of thousands.
¹⁴ May our cattle reproduce plentifully
  without miscarriage or loss.
  May there be no cries of distress in our
    streets.

¹⁵ Happy is the nation of whom this is
    true;
  happy are the people whose God is
    the LORD!

A Hymn of Praise*

145 I will proclaim your greatness,
my God and king;
I will thank you forever and ever.
2 Every day I will thank you;
I will praise you forever and ever.
3 The LORD is great and is to be highly
praised;
his greatness is beyond
understanding.

4 What you have done will be praised
from one generation to the next;
they will proclaim your mighty acts.
5 They will speak of your glory and
majesty,
and I will meditate on your
wonderful deeds.
6 People will speak of your mighty deeds,
and I will proclaim your greatness.
7 They will tell about all your goodness
and sing about your kindness.
8 The LORD is loving and merciful,
slow to become angry and full of
constant love.
9 He is good to everyone
and has compassion on all he made.

10 All your creatures, LORD, will praise
you,
and all your people will give you
thanks.
11 They will speak of the glory of your
royal power
and tell of your might,
12 so that everyone will know your mighty
deeds
and the glorious majesty of your
kingdom.
13 Your rule is eternal,
and you are king forever.

*HEBREW TITLE: *A song of praise by David.*

The LORD is faithful to his promises;
  he is merciful in all his acts.
14 He helps those who are in trouble;
  he lifts those who have fallen.

15 All living things look hopefully to you,
  and you give them food when they
    need it.
16 You give them enough
  and satisfy the needs of all.

17 The LORD is righteous in all he does,
  merciful in all his acts.
18 He is near to those who call to him,
  who call to him with sincerity.
19 He supplies the needs of those who
    honor him;
  he hears their cries and saves them.
20 He protects everyone who loves him,
  but he will destroy the wicked.

21 I will always praise the LORD;
  let all his creatures praise his holy
    name forever.

In Praise of God the Savior

146 Praise the LORD!
    Praise the LORD, my soul!
2 I will praise him as long as I live;
  I will sing to my God all my life.

3 Don't put your trust in human leaders;
  no human being can save you.
4 When they die, they return to the dust;
  on that day all their plans come to an
    end.

5 Happy is the man who has the God of
    Jacob to help him
  and who depends on the LORD his
    God,

⁶ the Creator of heaven, earth, and sea,
and all that is in them.
He always keeps his promises;
⁷ he judges in favor of the oppressed
and gives food to the hungry.

The LORD sets prisoners free
⁸ and gives sight to the blind.
He lifts those who have fallen;
he loves his righteous people.
⁹ He protects the strangers who live in
our land;
he helps widows and orphans,
but takes the wicked to their ruin.

And gives food to the hungry. (146.7)

¹⁰ The LORD is king forever.
 Your God, O Zion, will reign for all
  time.

Praise the LORD!

In Praise of God the Almighty

147 Praise the LORD!

It is good to sing praise to our God;
 it is pleasant and right to praise him.
² The LORD is restoring Jerusalem;
 he is bringing back the exiles.
³ He heals the broken-hearted
 and bandages their wounds.

⁴ He has decided the number of the stars
 and calls each one by name.
⁵ Great and mighty is our Lord;
 his wisdom cannot be measured.
⁶ He raises the humble,
 but crushes the wicked to the ground.

⁷ Sing hymns of praise to the LORD;
 play music on the harp to our God.
⁸ He spreads clouds over the sky;
 he provides rain for the earth
 and makes grass grow on the hills.
⁹ He gives animals their food
 and feeds the young ravens when
  they call.

¹⁰ His pleasure is not in strong horses,
 nor his delight in brave soldiers;
¹¹ but he takes pleasure in those who
  honor him,
 in those who trust in his constant
  love.

¹² Praise the LORD, O Jerusalem!
 Praise your God, O Zion!

¹³ He keeps your gates strong;
   he blesses your people.
¹⁴ He keeps your borders safe
   and satisfies you with the finest
     wheat.

¹⁵ He gives a command to the earth,
   and what he says is quickly done.
¹⁶ He spreads snow like a blanket
   and scatters frost like dust.
¹⁷ He sends hail like gravel;
   no one can endure the cold he sends!
¹⁸ Then he gives a command, and the ice
     melts;
   he sends the wind, and the water
     flows.

¹⁹ He gives his message to his people,
   his instructions and laws to Israel.
²⁰ He has not done this for other nations;
   they do not know his laws.

Praise the LORD!

A Call for the Universe to Praise God

148 Praise the LORD!

Praise the LORD from heaven,
   you that live in the heights above.
² Praise him, all his angels,
   all his heavenly armies.

³ Praise him, sun and moon;
   praise him, shining stars.
⁴ Praise him, highest heavens,
   and the waters above the sky.⁵

⁵ Let them all praise the name of the
     LORD!
   He commanded, and they were created;

⁵ WATERS ABOVE THE SKY: *See Genesis 1.6-7.*

⁶   by his command they were fixed in
        their places forever,
     and they cannot disobey.'

⁷ Praise the LORD from the earth,
     sea monsters and all ocean depths;
⁸ lightning and hail, snow and clouds,
     strong winds that obey his command.

⁹ Praise him, hills and mountains,
     fruit trees and forests;
¹⁰ all animals, tame and wild,
     reptiles and birds.

¹¹ Praise him, kings and all peoples,
     princes and all other rulers;
¹² girls and young men,
     old people and children too.

¹³ Let them all praise the name of the
        LORD!
     His name is greater than all others;
        his glory is above earth and heaven.
¹⁴ He made his nation strong,
     so that all his people praise him—
        the people of Israel, so dear to him.

Praise the LORD!

A Hymn of Praise

149 Praise the LORD!

Sing a new song to the LORD;
     praise him in the assembly of his
        faithful people!
² Be glad, Israel, because of your Creator;
     rejoice, people of Zion, because of
        your king!

' by his command . . . disobey; or he has fixed them in their places
for all time, by a command that lasts forever.

³ Praise his name with dancing;
    play drums and harps in praise of
      him.

⁴ The LORD takes pleasure in his people;
    he honors the humble with victory.
⁵ Let God's people rejoice in their
      triumph
    and sing joyfully all night long.
⁶ Let them shout aloud as they praise
      God,
    with their sharp swords in their
      hands
⁷   to defeat the nations
    and to punish the peoples;
⁸   to bind their kings in chains,
    their leaders in chains of iron;
⁹   to punish the nations as God has
      commanded.
This is the victory of God's people.

Praise the LORD!

Praise the LORD!

150 Praise the LORD!

Praise God in his Temple!
    Praise his strength in heaven!
² Praise him for the mighty things he has
      done.
    Praise his supreme greatness.

³ Praise him with trumpets.
    Praise him with harps and lyres.
⁴ Praise him with drums and dancing.
    Praise him with harps and flutes.
⁵ Praise him with cymbals.
    Praise him with loud cymbals.
⁶ Praise the LORD, all living creatures!

Praise the LORD!

Praise the LORD! (150.1)

MAPS

ANCIENT WORLD

PERSIAN
GULF

ELAM
Susa

Ecbatana

Lake
Urmia

Lake
Van

Umma

HURRIANS

Nineveh

ASSYRIA
Asshur

Tigris River

Nuzi

Accad?
ACCAD

Babylon
BABYLONIA

Nippur

Ur

MESOPOTAMIA

Euphrates River

Mari

Haran

Palmyra

ARABIAN
DESERT

Carchemish

HITTITES

TAURUS MTS.

Tarsus

Ugarit

Arvad

Gebal
(Byblos)

Sidon

Tyre

PHOENICIA

SYRIA
Hamath

Orontes R.

Kadesh

Damascus

KEDAR

Jordan River

Shechem
Jericho

Dor

Megiddo
CANAAN
Jerusalem
Hebron
Gaza
Beersheba

Dead Sea

Tamar

ARABAH

MIDIAN

Kadesh
Barnea

SINAI

RED
SEA

KITTIM
(CYPRUS)

MEDITERRANEAN
SEA

Heliopolis
GOSHEN

EGYPT

Nile R.

Memphis

Miles
0   250

Kms
0   250

Kadesh

MEDITERRANEAN SEA

Gebal

SIDONIANS LEBANON MTS.

BETH-REHOB

SYRIA

Sidon

• Damascus

Tyre

▲ MT HERMON

Abel • Dan

Hazor

MAACAH

Bashan

Cabul

GESHUR • Ashtaroth

MT CARMEL ▲

Megiddo

Edrei

Dor

Jezreel

Taanach

MT GILBOA

Jabesh

Ramoth

Shechem

Jordan R.

Zarethan

Jabbok

Gath-rimmon

Jazer

Joppa

Beth Horon

Bethel

Rabbah

Gezer

Jericho

AMMONITES

Ashdod

Ekron

Jerusalem

Heshbon

Ashkelon

PHILISTINES

Medeba

Gath?

Hebron

Dibon

Gaza

Debir

Dead Sea

Aroer

Gerar • Ziklag?

Beersheba •

MOABITES

Kir Heres

Tamar •

AMALEKITES

• Bozrah

• Kadesh Barnea

EDOMITES

• Sela

The Negev

The Desert

UNITED ISRAEL KINGDOM

0   Miles   60

0   Kms   60

© United Bible Societies, 1976

Eziongeber

GULF OF AQABA